The Addiction Ministry Handbook

The Addiction Ministry Handbook

A Guide for Faith Communities

Denis Meacham

Skinner House Books
Boston

Printed in the United States

Cover design by Suzanne Morgan
Text design by Communicáto, Ltd.

ISBN 1-55896-476-2

Library of Congress Cataloging-in-Publication Data
Meacham, Denis G.
   The addiction ministry handbook : a guide for faith communities / Denis G. Meacham.
      p. cm.
   Includes bibliographical references.
   ISBN 1-55896-476-2 (alk. paper)
   1. Church work with recovering addicts.   I. Title.

BV4460.3.M43 2004
259'.429—dc22
                                                          2004045377

Contents

Introduction   vii

The Basics about Addiction   1

The Spiritual Dimension   17

Recovery in a Faith Community   37

The Addiction Ministry Committee   47

Helping Special Populations   65

Helping the Family and Friends   93

Looking Forward   109

Resources   111

    Commonly Abused Substances   113

    Jellinek's Phases and Progression of Alcoholism   120

    The Twelve Steps of Alcoholics Anonymous   122

    Alcohol Abuse Assessment Tool   123

    Congregational Addiction Assessment Questionnaire 124

    For More Information   126

Acknowledgments   128

Index   129

Introduction

One Sunday, a minister stood in front of the congregation and invited anyone whose life had been seriously affected by addiction to come to the front of the sanctuary and light a candle of hope. As he stood there, knowing the statistics on addiction and understanding the damage that it can inflict on a user's friends and family, the minister wasn't sure how many people in the congregation would be willing to acknowledge their experience so publicly. But so many people came forward that at one point, the line moving toward the candles reached to the rear of the room. After the service, the minister counted the candles: Well over two-thirds of those attending the service had come forward. Since that day, he has used this ritual element in Sunday worship services many times and with similar results. On several occasions, virtually everyone in the pews has acknowledged a personal experience with addiction.

That minister was me, and I belong in that line of people coming forward to light a candle. After a downward spiral of around-the-clock drinking that lasted for years and finally left me incapable of going on with life without help, I ended up in a detoxification/rehabilitation hospital. The day I hit bottom marked the beginning of an odyssey of recovery, discovery, and new life. In the early stages of my treatment, I learned what I needed to do to stay sober and reclaim my life. I also learned that addiction is the great equalizer. My eight companions in treatment ranged in age from nineteen to seventy-two, in education from high school dropout to M.B.A., and in social standing from street person to high-ranking administrator in a city police department. They were male and female; gay and straight; white, Hispanic, and Asian. After only a few days in rehab, this disparate group bonded and showed a level of mutual care and respect that would have surprised many of us, had we encountered it outside the hospital. We came to understand the essential vulnerability of being human, and we learned that by pooling our strength, we might have enough to help all of us heal.

Two simple notions have formed the foundation of my recovery and my work. First, while addiction has physical, psychological, and social consequences, recovery is essentially a spiritual undertaking—a journey of reconnection to one's true self and deepest values as well as to others and to the life force, the source of good in the universe. In a religious sense, addiction can be understood as idolatry, and casting out the false idol is only the first step in recovering one's spiritual footing. The second foundation is that recovery takes place in community—a caring, supportive community of fellow substance abusers and committed, nonjudgmental caregivers who respect the worth and dignity of every individual.

My little group in rehab was my first recovery community. My second was Alcoholics Anonymous, and I grabbed on to AA's program and principles for dear life. The problem was that I couldn't spend all my time there. During my first weeks and months of sobriety, I paced the floor of my living room between meetings, trying to hold on until the next one. I remember wishing that my church—a vibrant Unitarian Universalist community in which my family and I had been active members for years—could have helped me. But there was nothing there for a recovering alcoholic nor at any of the many churches I explored over the next several years (other than AA meetings in their basements).

As my sobriety stabilized, I began to think about how my church could make a difference for the chemically dependent people following me into recovery. To this end, I "came out" in the pulpit as a recovering alcoholic, got trained as a lay minister, and began formal schoolwork in addiction treatment and services. Eventually, I started a recovery support group, provided pastoral counseling for chemically dependent people and their families, and earned certification as a drug/alcohol counselor. In 2000, First Parish in Brewster, Massachusetts, invited me to try out my ideas for a comprehensive, church-based addictions prevention and recovery support program. They gave me an office, my own telephone line, access to ministers, a staff, a pulpit, and other church resources. Together, we began to build a new kind of ministry. This book bears the fruit of that journey and the seeds for a much wider undertaking of this work in faith communities everywhere, regardless of theology.

The concept of an *addiction ministry* is not the province of any one religion or faith tradition. Unitarian Universalists embrace the commitment to support each individual's pursuit of his or her own spiritual truths and authorities, and this book is written in that spirit. For many people who turn to twelve-step programs, ideas about a higher power can be a formidable barrier to becoming fully engaged. Many people struggle with previously unquestioned assumptions from their religious traditions and teachings, and for them, approaching the challenge of addiction from a *spiritual* perspective, rather than a *religious* one, may be helpful in establishing a new basis for soulful engagement with the work of recovery.

This handbook is a guide and resource for faith communities committed to serving the special needs of their members whose lives have been touched by addiction—statistically more than half of any congregation. It is neither an exhaustive treatise on addiction science nor a superficial gloss of a very complicated subject. Instead, it is meant to provide both ministers and laypersons with a fundamental knowledge base for working effectively with people who have drug and alcohol problems. The literature on addiction work in faith communities is sparse. While there are several important works grounded in Protestant theology on the pastoral care of chemically dependent people, these do not focus on the church community. The few that are church oriented focus primarily on alcohol dependence and are addressed to the church pastor, assuming that he or she will be the primary force in initiating and sustaining this new work. This assumption may be the principal reason that so few churches offer an addiction ministry; namely, the commitment of time, energy, and attention required may simply be too much to ask from an already overburdened parish minister.

The driving force for establishing an addiction ministry must come from within the congregation and have the understanding, support, and occasional collaboration of the pastor. The pastor will be able to do much to advance this work, but the key to its success will lie in the devotion of a few church members who will learn how to tap the experience and authority of the pastor and initiate programs to support addiction recovery within their spiritual community. The church members who take up this work are typically in recovery themselves or have been touched deeply by addiction. These individuals are most likely to step forward to form an *addiction ministry committee (AMC)* and help build a program.

Throughout this book, the term *pastoral caregiver* is used to refer to anyone— minister or layperson, member of the AMC or other volunteer—who is an active participant in addiction ministry. The term thus distinguishes between individuals who provide services through the faith community and addiction professionals, who provide diagnosis, treatment, and aftercare planning in clinical settings. Indeed, the pastoral volunteer should recommend and support professional care for any church member who comes forward to seek help with substance abuse.

For an addiction ministry to succeed, it must create an atmosphere in which such an individual will feel safe and respected coming forward for help. To this end, the underlying objective of the ministry must be to transform the faith community into an open, accepting, and healing environment, in which the societal stigma attached to addiction has been removed. Such an environment is built on spiritual values and a belief in the innate worth and dignity of every human being.

To this end, participants in the addiction ministry can lead members of the congregation to examine and acknowledge their prejudices and stereotypes regarding the nature of addiction and those it affects. When a congregation succeeds in eliminating the stigma of addiction within its own community, it is ready to begin transformation of the larger community. And many transformed faith communities can change the world.

The Basics
about Addiction

If there is one thing you should know about people who abuse drugs and alcohol—something that should be in your head and your heart when you are in contact with them—it is this: In most important ways, they are just like you and me. They are bright people and not-so-bright people. They are outgoing and jovial, and they are introverted and somber. Most go to work every day to earn a living. Many have families, raise children, take care of aging parents, go to church, and generally manage to be responsible, at least in some areas of their lives—just like you and me.

Like you and me, these individuals are also trying to cope with all the challenges that life throws at them. Using drugs or alcohol is one of their coping mechanisms, one that many people use without ever getting into any trouble. But for substance abusers, this particular coping mechanism has itself become a life challenge or worse—a serious threat to their health and well-being, the integrity of their family, and the emotional stability of their loved ones. And a characteristic of the illness of addiction (in fact, the defining characteristic) is that despite the negative consequences of their drug-abusive behavior, these individuals are compelled to continue in this destructive pattern. No one has ever *chosen* to be a drug addict. No one *wants* to be a compulsive user of alcohol. Rather, chemically dependent people are stuck in a coping behavior that probably served them well at one time, briefly, and now they can't change without help.

As you get to know these people, you will learn that they are not monsters (or at least no more so than the rest of us). Everything they do, including all of their destructive behaviors, would probably make sense to you if you were in their shoes. This is to say that alcohol and drug abusers are more like us than they are different. Like us, they are trying to make their way in the world. The problem is, their life strategies aren't working anymore. Out of an abiding reverence for their worth and dignity as fellow human beings, we are called as pastoral caregivers to companion them on their journey. And as we do, we should take very seriously a mantra of Alcoholics Anonymous: "There but for fortune go you or I."

From the dawn of human history, people have used chemicals to change the way they feel or perceive the world around them. In today's society, such substances are ubiquitous, and most of us have experienced them in one form or another: in coffee and tea; in Coca Cola, Mountain Dew, and many other sodas; in Benadryl and other over-the-counter cold and allergy medications; in many prescription medications; in cigarettes and all other tobacco products; and in beer, wine, and distilled spirits. Then, of course, there are the illicit varieties, such as marijuana, cocaine, and heroin. Even if we haven't consumed these substances ourselves, we have likely been affected by someone else's use of them, such as being in an automobile with a drug- or alcohol-impaired driver or being in the presence of someone smoking cigarettes. A small but significant percentage of users of such psychoactive substances cause damage to themselves (and often to those around them), and some of these individuals become dependent on these substances.

Dependence is reflected in a variety of changes in the individual, one of which involves changes in the brain. Substances of abuse interact with the brain's chemical neurotransmitters, which carry nerve impulses from one nerve cell to another. The release of certain neurotransmitters at nerve-cell endings, primarily in the limbic area of the brain, makes us feel good. Psychoactive substances affect the brain's neurochemistry by increasing the release of these neurotransmitters, by prolonging their presence at the nerve-cell endings, or by substituting for them—any of which results in the mood change sought in drug use. (It is interesting to note that certain conventional behaviors, such as accomplishing a difficult task, and certain physical activities, such as long-distance running, can also release these "feel good" chemicals in the brain, producing a so-called natural high.) When the psychoactive substance is gone from the brain, the effect stops.

For some people—and unfortunately, we cannot predict just which ones—the regular use of psychoactive substances will have an insidious effect. Over time, these individuals' brain chemistry, adjusting to repeated doses of the substance, will change, and the substance will become a necessary component of their new brain chemistry. At that point, they will need to use the drug to feel normal. Over time, more and more of the substance will be needed to maintain the same level of altered feeling (*tolerance*), and if the substance is withheld, the brain will signal its distress with painful symptoms throughout the body (*withdrawal*) as well as its need for more of the substance (*craving*).

This is the *physical* state of chemical dependence, in which external causes are no longer the principal impetus to drug use. The dependent person returns to the drug again and again because of a neurochemical need. Thus, the plight of the dependent individual is that he or she seeks drugs not so much to produce euphoria as to fight off the painful withdrawal that comes after the effects of the last drug use begin to wear off. As an alcohol-dependent patient in detoxification once said, "The only problem with addiction is that you can't stay high all the time."

Throughout time and across cultures, societies have distinguished between people who can use mood-altering substances in culturally acceptable ways and those who cannot. In modern times, the statistics reflecting drug and alcohol use have remained relatively consistent. For instance, according to Marc Galanter and Herbert Kleber, authors of *Textbook of Substance Abuse Treatment*, between 8 and 10 percent of the population have a drug or alcohol disorder at any given time in the United States. Moreover, between 15 and 20 percent of the population will experience a substance use problem sometime in their lives. Among adolescents ages fourteen through seventeen, the percentage of serious problem drinkers is estimated to be as high as 20 percent. Meanwhile, research has shown that each chemically dependent person has a serious negative impact on at least four family members. (The number of affected lives would surely be much higher if good friends, co-workers, and others were counted as well.) In sum, roughly half of the U.S. population is directly affected by substance abuse or dependence.

Other statistics dramatically fill in this picture of an insidious national health problem:

- The National Council on Alcoholism and Drug Dependence (NCADD) estimates that 43 percent of adults in the United States have experienced alcohol dependence in their family; that is, they grew up with an alcohol-dependent person, married one, or had an alcohol-dependent relative.
- One in eight Americans today is the child of an alcohol-dependent parent, estimates Trish Merrill in *Committed, Caring Communities*.
- As many as one in four people admitted to a general hospital (and one in three admitted to a Veterans Administration hospital) is an alcohol abuser or undiagnosed alcohol-dependent individual who is being treated for a problem connected to his or her substance abuse, according to NCADD.

- J. McGinnis and W. Foege write in the *Journal of the American Medical Association* that some 100,000 deaths a year in the United States can be traced to alcohol, which makes alcohol use the third-leading cause of preventable mortality (after tobacco use and diet/activity patterns).
- Jean Kinney and Gwen Leaton estimate in *Loosening the Grip* that 80 percent of substance-dependent people are not receiving any professional care.
- Despite widespread negative stereotypes about people with drug and alcohol problems, the vast majority of them (as many as 95 percent, according to one estimate) are employed or employable.
- In a large national survey by NCADD, 30 percent of children in grades four through six reported that they have been pressured by classmates to drink beer, 31 percent reported that they have been pressured to try marijuana, and 34 percent reported that they have been pressured to smoke cigarettes.

These statistics should be sobering, in every sense of the word. They are powerful testimony to the enormity of this too often silent problem of substance use and dependence.

Why People Start Using Drugs and Alcohol

Like almost every aspect of substance use, the reasons people choose to use drugs and alcohol are the subject of debate, theorizing, and research, both historical and modern. Prominent among the many explanations offered by experts are a desire to relieve stress, to heighten one's sense of personal control and power, to achieve a spiritual or mystical experience, to self-medicate for undiagnosed depression or anxiety or other debilitating emotional problems, to fit in with one's adolescent peers, and to conform to cultural or family patterns of substance use.

While each of these explanations has its advocates, the consensus today is that a person begins to use drugs or alcohol as a result of a combination of factors. The same can be said about people who, having tried drugs or alcohol once, develop an abusive or dependent pattern of use. All of the theories and studies notwithstanding, it may be as simple as this: People use drugs and alcohol because doing so quickly and effortlessly changes how they feel and therefore how they experience their surroundings and circumstances. It makes them feel good. Whether the problem is stress, anxiety, boredom, social unease, or a sense of powerlessness, after a couple of beers, everything seems fine! And a seemingly endless array of advertisements for alcohol remind us that pleasurable feelings and circumstances can be heightened by taking a drink or two. Indeed, since no one starts out using drugs or alcohol believing that he or she will become chemically dependent, perhaps the question should be, Why doesn't everybody become addicted to these "feel good" substances?

For so-called social drinkers, the typical effect of having a drink or two is mild euphoria. But for certain individuals, the effects of having even a single drink seem to be qualitatively different. Regardless of why they start to drink, these individuals seem destined for trouble with alcohol use. For them, consuming even a small amount of alcohol has profound effects. They report feeling "complete" or "whole," often for the first time in their lives. And from the beginning of their drinking history, they can tolerate more alcohol than their friends who only drink socially. The sought-after effect of substance use in these people is the creation of what they describe as a feeling of "rightness" or "completeness." In fact, some individuals may use mood-altering substances to fill a spiritual rather than a biological or psychological void.

Most people who experiment with psychoactive substances never move beyond social or recreational substance use. For others, their first experience with drugs or alcohol initiates a progressively serious attachment to mood-altering substances and behaviors, ultimately leading to abuse or dependence. While the particulars of this progression vary from individual to individual, the general pattern of deterioration in thinking and behavior that marks the loss of control over drug or alcohol use is sadly predictable. Understanding this pattern will not only make us as pastoral caregivers more sensitive to the needs of substance abusers, but it will also provide us with a tool to help individuals make sense of the often bewildering downward spiral of their lives or the lives of their loved ones. Such an understanding can be a strong motivator for voluntary behavior change or for seeking professional help.

The classic description of this progression in reference to alcohol was developed over forty years ago by the Reverend Vernon E. Johnson, an Episcopal priest, recovering alcoholic, and addiction treatment innovator. Johnson described four stages of drug use, the first of which is *experimentation*. In this first stage, the individual becomes familiar with both the euphoria and the relief from pain that drug use can produce. The experimenter learns that he or she can trust the drug to produce the desired effects upon each use and that he or she can modify or regulate the effects by adjusting how much of the drug is consumed.

Experimentation is followed by stage two, which involves *occasional use* of the substance. The user begins a pattern of regular, controlled use of the drug. In the case of alcohol, we would call this *appropriate* or *social use*. The user develops rules for when and where and how much to use and sticks to them. Thus, over the course of stages one and two, the user is developing a bond with the substance, one based on expecting a desired effect and trusting that the drug will deliver it. The user is also learning that he or she doesn't have to tolerate the discomforts of life, whether physical, psychological, or spiritual. When they feel the need, occasional users can profoundly change how they experience life. And since they have learned to trust the source of the altered state, anticipating the drug's effects may become a mood lifter in itself.

In the transition into stage three, the drug user's attachment to the substance begins to overpower any ability to control when, where, and how much he or she uses the substance. Loss of control produces behaviors and consequences that lead to growing feelings of guilt and shame. In this stage, the dependent user develops tolerance for the drug (the need for an ever-increasing amount to achieve the desired effects), and his or her increasing need leads to an all-powerful preoccupation with locating, acquiring, using, and hiding the drug and with protecting its source. During this stage, the user's physical and psychological health begins to noticeably deteriorate and he or she faces mounting negative consequences in family, social, and vocational life.

In the last stage, described by Johnson as using the drug "to feel normal," the user turns to the substance in an increasingly fruitless attempt to relieve the wretchedness of withdrawal. The drug is now an absolute requirement for feeling normal, and many users in this stage do not even experience a pleasing euphoria. Judging by the experiences of members of Alcoholics Anonymous, this is the stage that often leads to jail, a mental institution, or death—or recovery, if the user finally seeks help.

In Johnson's model, the alcohol (or drug) user has become chemically dependent by the third stage, during which attachment to the substance becomes the dominant reality of his or her life. According to neurobiologists, there has been such a fundamental change in brain chemistry by this stage that the addictive substance is now a physical need. The body's demand for it is as powerful as that for food. If the substance is withheld, the body will react with withdrawal symptoms that, depending on the abused substance, can range in effect from extreme discomfort to life-threatening seizures. In stage-four dependence, the power of the drug over the body and the mind is all consuming and thus devastating.

Another early approach to understanding the progression of alcohol dependence is found in the work of E. M. Jellinek. In his seminal text *The Disease Concept of Alcoholism,* published in 1960, Jellinek identified the associated signs and symptoms of four successive phases in the development of alcohol dependence. Jellinek captured both the progressive nature of alcohol dependence and the array of symptoms and experiences that characterize that progression. (See page 120 for a list of specific symptoms and experiences.) This information can be useful to the pastoral caregiver as an educational tool in working with alcohol- and drug-dependent people who don't want to see the connection between their alcohol- or drug-related experiences and their alcohol or drug use.

In describing the typical progression from experimentation with drugs and alcohol to abuse and dependence, Jellinek (like Johnson) suggested that moderate alcohol use in some people will develop into heavy and problematic use. And approximately one in three of these people will eventually become alcohol dependent, although exactly which people cannot be predicted. Jellinek also suggested (as did Johnson) that a series of warning signs typically indicate that someone's alcohol use is heading in a dangerous direction. But some individuals leapfrog over many of these signs on the way to dependence, whereas others exhibit most of them but never become chemically dependent. Research has shown that many people's drug or alcohol use moves predictably from alcohol and tobacco to marijuana and then to narcotics and finally to multiple-substance use. Yet some people who use cocaine have never used marijuana.

Neither the Johnson nor the Jellinek model suggests a causal relationship between the steps or phases. Progression is not inevitable, in other words. Instead, the models simply describe patterns of behavior in large groups of individuals.

Finally, one cautionary note regarding the causes or progression of substance use and dependence: Understanding how one came to be dependent on drugs or alcohol is rarely useful in helping an individual to change behaviors and effectively participate in recovery programs. Discussions that begin "How can I be an alcoholic when I never . . . ?" tend to divert attention from the signs and symptoms of existing problems and their implications for pastoral care and/or professional treatment.

Recognizing Chemical Dependence

People who abuse drugs and alcohol exhibit signs and symptoms of their illness that are relatively consistent and predictable. However, for several reasons, the diagnosis of chemical abuse or dependence is often difficult and ambiguous. Whereas a physical examination and laboratory tests can determine the presence and nature of a given medical condition, such as diabetes, the evidence for a diagnosis of chemical dependence primarily is found in a person's history of certain behaviors and psychological and social experiences. The drug or alcohol user may deny or rationalize these signs of disorder, complicating a diagnosis. Especially at the boundary between heavy use and abuse or between abuse and chemical dependence, employing even the most refined diagnostic tools will not always yield a clear conclusion.

The medical community generally recognizes the following levels of chemical use: nonuse, light to moderate use, heavy use, problematic use or abuse, and dependence. In order to standardize more precise terminology and because of the negative social connotations of much of the language in this field, the use of such terms as *alcoholism* and *addiction* has become less common. The preferred term is *substance dependence;* alcoholism and addiction are considered *dependencies.* The term *problematic use* is used to describe involvement with drugs and/or alcohol that results in significant problems but falls short of dependence. *Problematic substance use* is thus analogous to *substance abuse* in the older terminology, although this latter term is still widely used to describe any amount of substance use that produces negative consequences.

While the criteria for diagnosing substance dependence have undergone subtle refinements in recent years, the three widely accepted standards that must be met to establish a clinical diagnosis of substance dependence are loss of control, including repeated unsuccessful attempts to be abstinent; repeated experiences of negative consequences, such as health, family, and employment problems; and tolerance and/or withdrawal symptoms, including the need for a drink to get rid of a hangover.

Unfortunately, real life isn't usually as simple or predictable as this discussion might suggest. No one becomes chemically dependent the first time he or she uses a psychoactive substance, and most people who become social drinkers (and many who are occasional drug users) do not progress to substance abuse or dependence. Even among those people who do, the progression isn't always predictable or irreversible. A heavy user, for instance, may return to more moderate use or remain a heavy user for his or her entire life. On the other hand, especially with the multiple-drug (or *polysubstance*) use that is now so commonly seen in young people, it's quite possible for a person to move very quickly from casual drug or alcohol use to dependence.

For the pastoral caregiver, the following simple, operational definition of *addiction* can be very useful: A person is addicted to a substance if, after using the substance, he or she experiences an increase in serious negative consequences of his or her substance use but does not stop. Quite simply, if the individual were not *compelled* to use the substance, he or she would not risk more negative consequences. While this definition lacks the detail and nuance of the medical definition of chemical *dependence,* it captures the characteristic freedomless, self-destructive behavior of the dependent person.

The essential question we as pastoral caregivers must ask ourselves in regard to helping a troubled church member is this: Is the use of drugs or alcohol causing serious problems in this person's life? For instance, a common situation encountered by pastoral counselors is one in which a couple seeks help because one partner is disturbed by the other's drinking. The drinker may deny problematic alcohol use, but the very fact that he or she has not reduced or stopped drinking in response to his or her partner's concern and that this issue has brought the couple to counseling points to a substance abuse problem, according to our simple definition. If drug or alcohol use is causing a problem, that person (or couple) needs help. Such an individual often must be provided with educational information to help make the connections between his or her substance use and family, social, employment, and other problems. If the individual denies the connections or is unable to change his or her behavior even after acknowledging the connections, he or she is a candidate for further assessment by a substance use professional.

While our operational definition of *addiction* does not require us to establish *problematic* or *dependent* drug or alcohol use or to distinguish between the two, it represents the defining characteristics of addictive behavior. As such, it can serve us well as pastoral caregivers in making an initial (albeit tentative) assessment of a drug or alcohol problem.

The Disease Model of Chemical Dependence

As noted earlier, people throughout history have used mood-altering substances for social, medical, and religious purposes. And undoubtedly, from the beginning of time, some people have abused these substances, becoming a source of harm to themselves and those around them. Depending on the time and the culture, the misuse of or overindulgence in psychoactive substances has provoked a variety of responses, from amusement to disgust, moral outrage, and even social or legal sanction.

The medical community in the Western world became officially concerned with the compulsive use of chemical substances relatively recently. Yet even today, several decades after the American Medical Association categorized chemical dependence as a *disease,* the debate continues over whether chemical dependence should be understood and treated as such. There are still people today who believe that substance dependence stems from a lack of moral fiber or willpower. Others argue that addiction is social, psychological, or behavioral (or a combination of these), rather than biological, and is thus not a disease. Nonetheless, arguments for the retention of the disease model are several and persuasive. Most important, acceptance of this model has served to reduce the stigma associated with chemical dependence, thereby making it easier for people struggling with abuse and dependence to seek professional help.

Meanwhile, the psychological, social, and spiritual needs of people in recovery are real and ever present. Once the body has been detoxified and any medical problems resulting from drug use have been attended to, healing in these other nonbiological aspects of life is what constitutes recovery and makes stable sobriety possible. Indeed, the narrowness of conventional medicine's disease focus, rather than any deficiency in the disease concept of addiction, may be responsible for the fact that the most effective interventions for addiction are *nonmedical.* But our understanding of the nature of the illness is evolving. A biopsychosocial understanding of disease is emerging in contemporary medicine, and nowhere can it be more usefully applied than to the illness of chemical dependence. Meanwhile, the disease model seems to offer the chemically dependent individual and society as a whole more positives than negatives, certainly compared with the less popular and less well supported alternatives that have been proffered to date.

The Stages of Change

Dependent individuals usually come into treatment with a variety of biological, psychological, social, and spiritual problems caused by their compulsive use of drugs or alcohol. Some of these problems can be dealt with medically and resolved fairly quickly. Others will take more time and require the attention of nonmedical specialists. One such issue is the compulsive behavior that is a hallmark of addiction. Recovery from chemical dependence demands changing addictive behaviors, and maintaining long-term, stable recovery means learning how to prevent relapse to those old destructive behaviors.

People have used a variety of tools to help them change unhealthy behaviors, but until recently, the change process itself received little attention. As it turns out, successful change may not be the result of a simple, one-step decision to alter behavior. Instead, people seem to go through a series of stages in the change process, and negotiating each stage is critical not only to continued progress but ultimately to a successful outcome.

This new understanding of the change process is largely due to the innovative work of James Prochaska and colleagues at the University of Rhode Island. Their studies led them to develop a model that describes six stages in the change process along with the reasons so many people fail to change unwanted behaviors. According to this now widely influential model, while people often regress, working through each stage is necessary for change to be successful.

The first stage in the change process is *precontemplation.* Individuals in this stage are not ready for change. In the grips of denial, they resist the notion that their drug or alcohol use is a problem. As far as they are concerned, their problems can be traced to the behaviors of others. And so while they may argue the need for these others to change, they will resist any discussion of their own need to do so and avoid feedback that might point in that direction. For many precontemplators, this resistance to change is accompanied by *demoralization,* or the feeling that change isn't possible. This suggests that they realize they are in trouble but are not capable of taking responsibility for the situation they find themselves in. This demoralization may ultimately work to these individuals' advantage in moving them from the first to the second stage of change.

People in the *contemplation* stage have begun to break through their denial of the serious problems in their lives and to take personal responsibility. But while they may recognize the need for change, they are not yet ready to act upon this awareness. Contemplators often come to understand not only their problems but also the steps required for change. However, they often become stuck at this stage, unable to take action.

In the third stage, *preparation,* people begin planning the actions they need to take, but the ambiguity of the precontemplation stage may persist. Thus, their first attempts to take action may be half-hearted and inconclusive. In fact, these individuals may still be trying to convince themselves that they are really ready to change. At this point in the change process, it can be very helpful for individuals to let others know of their intention to change.

During the *action* stage, people actually make changes, both in their old behaviors and in the environment that has supported those behaviors. Since this is the stage in which individuals' efforts to change are most observable, this is also when they are likely to receive the most encouragement. There can be serious consequences, however, in caregivers focusing their support just on this stage. The critical earlier steps leading to action and the equally important and often most difficult post-action stage of maintaining the new healthier behaviors may go unacknowledged, thereby sabotaging the entire effort. It is important to appreciate that there are different requirements for the negotiation of each stage and that progress depends on the completion of the necessary tasks in each stage.

In stage five, *maintenance,* individuals learn how to prevent relapse to their old behaviors and how to incorporate these preventive measures into their daily lives. For some people, this stage lasts a lifetime. Without a commitment to maintenance, people will almost certainly relapse to the precontemplation or contemplation stage and thus to their old behaviors. Not having a program for the maintenance of new behaviors often proves the undoing of fad diets and other schemes for lifestyle change that promise quick and easy results.

In the final stage, *termination,* individuals have left their old behaviors permanently behind them and no longer face temptations to relapse. The notion here is that individuals who reach this stage can confidently proceed with their lives without any further attention to change maintenance. They have completed the process of change.

It is important to remember that Prochaska's stages of change model is designed to encompass a wide variety of behaviors. In his work, he touches on people's attempts to make changes in such problem areas as obesity, juvenile delinquency, depression, interpersonal problems, cigarette smoking, emotional problems, overexposure to the sun, and heroin dependence. It seems reasonable to believe that a person could change some behaviors without having a permanent maintenance program in place to avoid relapse. However, nearly all substance abuse experts believe that chemical dependence is a chronic, life-threatening, relapsing illness. Prudence would suggest attending to the maintenance of one's sobriety throughout life.

The stages of change model has become a powerful resource for treatment providers in the addictive disorders, and its components should be understood by anyone working with dependent people. The model teaches three fundamental principles of change that pastoral caregivers should understand in working with people who have substance use problems.

First, while the six stages of change are sequential, progress from one to the next is not necessarily or even usually linear. People often regress to earlier stages, in which case the work of change needs to begin anew. Second, individuals cannot successfully do the work of one particular stage until they have completed the work of all previous stages. According to Prochaska, this is why so many action-oriented programs for behavioral change are unsuccessful; that is, the requisite foundational work has not been attended to.

Third, our job as pastoral caregivers is to deal with people where they are, not where we would like them to be. If an individual does not believe he or she has a drug or alcohol problem or is not willing to take responsibility for his or her actions, we are almost certainly not going to convince that person to enter a chemical dependence detox or rehab program. The drug- or alcohol-abusing person at the precontemplation stage is not ready for change. However, we may very well be able to help him or her with other problems that often accompany the chemical-dependent lifestyle, such as serious health issues. Meeting people where they are means honoring their worth and dignity as human beings, regardless of the circumstances they find themselves in. Helping precontemplators can also create trust and a bond between them and the helping community. This will prove valuable when they are ready to make other more difficult changes in their lives.

Finally, although motivational counselors use a variety of skills and strategies to help move precontemplators to consider change, the basic technique involves increasing their awareness of the connection between the problems they are having and their drug or alcohol use. As pastoral caregivers, we can certainly weave this strategy into our caring interactions with individuals. Overall, an understanding of the stages of change model makes it possible for pastoral caregivers to support individuals in setting realistic, achievable goals on their journey toward health and well-being.

Getting a sense of an individual's readiness for change can be part of an overall pastoral evaluation of any church member seeking advice or help for a drug or alcohol problem. Determining what stage of change a person is in will suggest the sort of care and support he or she will need. More and more substance abuse professionals are being trained in motivating clients to move from precontemplation to contemplation of behavior changes. Referral to such a professional may be the appropriate next step for individuals who are not ready to change their problematic behaviors but are willing to explore the causes of their growing problems. Regardless, when a pastoral caregiver is satisfied that an individual is engaging in problematic substance use, he or she should consider a referral for professional assessment and treatment.

Alcoholics Anonymous

Alcoholics Anonymous (AA) and such derivative twelve-step programs as Narcotics Anonymous (NA), Cocaine Anonymous (CA), Overeaters Anonymous (OA), and Gamblers Anonymous (GA) are the cornerstones of long-term, stable recovery for many people with chemical or behavioral dependence. The beginnings of AA can be traced to a meeting between two alcoholics*—Bill Wilson, a New York stockbroker, and Dr. Bob Smith, a physician—at Smith's home in Akron, Ohio, in 1935. Over the next several years, AA groups were started elsewhere in Ohio and in New York, and by 1939, over one hundred alcoholics had found sobriety through affiliation with the program. AA now has over two million members around the world, about two-thirds of whom are men.

Author's note: Throughout this section, I use such terms as *alcoholic* and *alcoholism* because these are the terms used by AA.

The essential premise of recovery in AA is that it is not enough for someone to stop drinking to maintain sobriety and lead a productive, fulfilling life. An alcoholic must make fundamental changes in his or her life. To promote such change, personal shortcomings and character defects (as they are referred to in the AA literature) are uncovered in the process of undertaking AA's Twelve Steps of recovery (see page 122), Unless he or she makes such changes, the nondrinking alcoholic will probably experience what AA calls a "dry drunk," which can be as tormenting as active alcoholism and usually leads to a return to alcoholic drinking. The power of the Twelve Steps to facilitate personal change is reflected in the millions of people who have turned their lives around through participation in AA.

Another tenet of recovery in AA is that to maintain sobriety, the alcoholic individual needs to pass on the benefits of the program to others struggling with addiction by helping them embrace the Twelve Steps. This represents one aspect of the all-important service component of the program, which is embodied in the Twelfth Step.

At present, over fifty-thousand AA meetings are held each week in the United States. In large urban areas, several meetings are usually held on any given day. Many meetings are open not only to AA members but also to their families and friends as well as interested members of the public. Other meetings are restricted to members of AA. There are also meetings organized solely for women, for newcomers, for gays and lesbians, and for members of other demographic and affinity groups. Local-area AA service offices and meetings themselves make lists available that show the times, locations, and types of meetings available. There are three basic meeting formats: *speaker meetings,* in which members invited from another meeting group tell their personal stories; *discussion groups,* in which each AA member in attendance is given the opportunity to speak; and *Twelve-Step meetings,* in which members read and discuss one of the Twelve Steps.

The past several decades have seen a rise in polysubstance abuse, especially among young people. It follows that the people who typically come to AA today have life histories that include both drugs and alcohol. AA's only membership restriction in this regard is that alcohol must be one of the person's abused substances.

Another foundational element of AA and other twelve-step recovery programs is *sponsorship,* in which new members are taken under the wings of more experienced members to help them learn how to use the various components of the program and get the most out of it. AA emphasizes the importance of members asking for help from their sponsors and other members, especially when first starting out. Beginners are encouraged to get phone numbers from group members so they can make contact outside of meetings for advice and help in maintaining their sobriety.

The core teachings of AA are presented in a book entitled *Alcoholics Anonymous: The Story of How Many Men and Women Have Recovered from Alcoholism,* which is referred to in the program simply as the "Big Book." Recently reissued in a fourth edition, it has been one of the top-ten best-selling books worldwide for decades and is essential reading for any pastoral caregiver committed to working with substance-dependent people. AA also makes available to members a wide array of books and pamphlets about recovery, and many AA members become daily readers of inspirational AA literature. AA members are also exposed to a variety of often repeated slogans, such as "One step at a time," "Easy does it," "Keep it simple," "Live and let live," and "Let go and let God." Deceptively simple and even trite sounding at first glance, many of these slogans represent age-old wisdom that can be easily grasped and quickly recollected to invoke the essence of the twelve-step approach to life.

The success of AA in fostering stable recovery from alcohol dependence is unrivaled and well documented. In addition to twelve-step programs that focus on various addictive substances and behaviors, there are programs for family members and loved ones of substance-dependent people, such as Al-Anon for adults and Alateen for children. One of the simplest and most important initiatives a church community can take to respond to the needs of dependent individuals is to host weekly meetings of one or more such twelve-step programs.

Avowed atheists, people with no formal religious beliefs, and some members of liberal faith communities are sometimes put off by AA's religious overtones. While AA emphasizes in its literature that it is a *spiritual* program, not a *religious* one, discussions of a higher power are often couched in "God talk," and it is not unusual for AA members to recite the Lord's Prayer at the close of a meeting. One of the challenges of pastoral caregivers is to help people in recovery overcome this and other barriers to full participation in twelve-step programs. The experience of many addiction counselors has shown that the so-called religion issue is often a red herring that masks other more fundamental reasons for resistance.

Any barrier to the effective application of twelve-step recovery principles can usually be negotiated with thoughtful counseling. Even when reasoning seems to fail, the argument can be made that a patient won't refuse prescribed medication for a medical illness because he or she doesn't like the taste of the medicine or understand why it is effective. (In other words, the substance-dependent person does not have to enjoy the principles and practices of AA to commit to the program.) AA is one of the few proven "medicines" for the illness of alcohol dependence, and people need to be supported in taking their medicine, even if they find it disagreeable.

When resistance to twelve-step programs simply cannot be overcome, individuals can be referred to any of several self-help programs that have been organized to accommodate objections to components (especially the spiritual ones) of the AA program model. Such groups as SMART Recovery, Secular Organizations for Sobriety (SOS), and Secular Sobriety Groups (SSG) have attempted to meet this need for alternative programs. While comparatively little evidence is available of these programs' effectiveness at helping people maintain sobriety and the availability of their meetings in any given locale may be sparse or nonexistent, referral to such groups should not be discounted for individuals who otherwise will have no self-help group support in their recovery.

The Spiritual Dimension

Life would be a lot simpler if we human beings could move down a rung or two on the phylogenetic ladder and become part of the animal world. Animals presumably are not perplexed or tormented by their existence nor do they seek its meaning. But we are and we do. We are confused, mystified, and often frustrated and made anxious by the world we inhabit and by the beyond that we imagine.

Certainly, part of the explanation behind this conflict is the fact that we are mortal, something that's been observed and lamented by philosophers, priests, and poets since the beginning of time. We are all going to die, and no accomplishment can save us from that physical nonexistence. Uneasiness, even despair over our mortality has been an ageless companion, begging the question of how and where we can find meaning in our brief existence.

As human beings, we also have the capacity to imagine beyond the limits of mortal existence. The paradox that stems from the uneasy coexistence of our mortality and our self-transcendence has been described by many theologians as the uniquely human existential circumstance. It both elicits and defines our spiritual or religious response to life. This response represents our conviction that there is something larger and longer lasting, more fundamental and important than our transitory existence, something that gives it meaning. At different times and in different cultures, this essential reality has been differently described and understood, but whatever its form, it is that which demands our ultimate commitment and the reality from which we derive our most deeply held values. Moreover, it is our source of strength and hope in the face of the fallibility of our humanity. However understood, it is the substance of our faithfulness.

We turn to faith for the strength to live with our mortality. But it is not just our mortality that confounds us. There are forces at work in our individual lives that are beyond our understanding and control. Our ability to cope with the unexpected, the unfulfilling, the traumatic realities of daily existence often depends on our spiritual resources.

The fundamental question we each must ask is, To what belief or beliefs are we faithful? Is the substance of our faith good (that is, life affirming and sustaining), or is it bad (evil and destructive)? As Unitarian Universalist theologian James Luther Adams reminds us, *all* human beings are faithful. Even the Nazis had faith—faith in Hitler's power and vision of Aryan domination of the world. Viktor Frankl, in *Man's Search for Meaning,* his extraordinary account of his daily struggle to survive in a concentration camp, discovered his faith in the inextinguishable and transformative power of love. He discovered that what life asked of him was to be in touch with his faith, and the act of responsibility to his faith was to survive his ordeal and be reunited with his beloved wife. His faith in the power of love, specifically the love of his wife, gave meaning to his otherwise wretched existence. Just as importantly, his faith was the one thing his persecutors couldn't take from him.

We are all faithful to some belief. The Christian believes in the redemptive grace of God, as manifested in the acts and teachings of Jesus Christ. The Moslem believes in the rule of Allah and the divinely inspired words of the prophet Mohammad that form the Koran. Many Unitarian Universalists are humanists, who place their faith in science and the ingenuity and collective commitment of responsible human beings to better the lot of humankind. What does faithfulness to an ultimate commitment or a deeply held value do for us as individuals? Certainly, it does not eliminate the hardships or existential anxieties of life. However, it may allow us to tolerate them as necessary contrasts to the good and joyous aspects of life. For many of us, our faith is transformative, capable of bringing us beyond toleration of life's pain to experience its true meaningfulness.

In sum, we all have faith. This faith, embodied in our commitment to our most deeply held values and beliefs, gives meaning to our lives. That in which we have faith is that for which we would give our lives. Our spirituality is the part of our being that calls us to honor our faith, continually examine it, and live according to the deeply held values our examined faith embraces.

At least since the founding of AA and perhaps before, we have understood the phenomenon of addiction to have biological, psychological, and social and spiritual components. AA, the most successful recovery regime to date, is avowedly a spiritual program. And so it seems curious that the spiritual dimension has been relatively unexamined. Our spiritual dimension is about what is most profoundly important to us in our lives—our faithfulness to an ultimate source of hope, joy, and solace. Addiction represents a disruption in this spiritual grounding. As such, addiction could be called a *disordered spiritual attachment.*

When someone is addicted, he or she becomes attached to a harmful behavior or substance and can longer exercise free will in the choice of performing that behavior or consuming that substance. He or she does something; there are serious, harmful consequences; and he or she does it again. The addict does it again even when he or she doesn't want to because he or she has to. In an all too common and painful scenario, millions of alcohol-dependent people woke up yesterday morning with a numbing hangover and vowed not to drink that day. Trembling, they dressed for work and went off to their jobs as lawyers, laborers, aerospace technicians, kindergarten teachers, store clerks, and physicians. This morning, they awoke feeling sick again and full of remorse because they could not abstain from drinking yesterday.

In his letter to the Romans, the apostle Paul says, "I do not understand my own actions. For I do not do what I want, but I do the very thing I hate. . . . I can will what is right, but I cannot do it. For I do not do the good I want, but the evil I do not want is what I do." Paul is talking about *attachment*—compulsive attachment to what is harmful and evil. In Paul's theology, the word for this attachment to evil is *sin.* Sin is removed by a voluntary reconnection to what is ultimately good—what is redemptive of health and wholeness and thus life affirming. The essence of the human predicament is found in the nature of our attachments and our freedom to choose them.

Mood-altering substances, power, pleasure, possessions—any of these and more can serve as a "higher power" in terms of becoming an object of ultimate commitment and expectation and providing a repository of hope for an existence free from the ambiguity of our mortality. At least momentarily, any of these objects of devotion can give us a feeling of satisfaction or completeness. But that feeling will not endure. The problem is that none of these objects acknowledges or embraces our dual nature as material and transcendent beings. They are the stuff of mortal existence and therefore impermanent, like us. Any satisfaction objects such as these provide will be transitory and undependable because they can be denied to us or taken away from us. In appealing to only half of our nature, they deny the other half.

These objects are therefore the stuff of *evil* faith because the compulsive pursuit of them makes us sick in body, mind, and spirit and virtually always traumatizes our loved ones as well. They are the stuff of evil faith because they overwhelm our capacity for love, compassion, honesty, and unselfishness. Only what is good and freely chosen can be deeply sustaining; no object of compulsive desire can feed the soul. All such solutions to our fundamental spiritual dilemma become false idols. In fact, their compulsive pursuit can look a lot like a religion gone horribly awry—idolatry. In his book *Dynamics of Faith*, Protestant theologian Paul Tillich describes an ultimate concern whose content proves to be temporal and dangerously useless:

> The inescapable consequence of idolatrous faith is "existential disappointment," a disappointment which penetrates into the very existence of man! This is the dynamics of idolatrous faith, and as such, the centered act of a personality; that the centering point is something which is more or less on the periphery; and that, therefore, the act of faith leads to a loss of the center and to a disruption of the personality. . . . For if it [one's ultimate concern] proves to be a failure, the meaning of one's life breaks down; one surrenders oneself, including truth and justice, to something which is not worth it.

The Spiritual Progression of Dependence

We examined Vernon Johnson's model of the biological, psychological, and social aspects of the spiral from drug or alcohol use to abuse and dependence in Chapter 1. In this chapter, we will construct a parallel four-stage model to address the spiritual progression of dependence, which can be seen in the gradual eclipsing of an individual's core meaning and values. Just as compulsive substance use consumes the individual's body and mind, so does it co-opt the life-affirming force at the center of his or her being, which sustains his or her growth toward wholeness and well-being.

In stage one of the spiritual progression to dependence, *experimentation* with mood-altering substances provides the individual with a chemical source of heightened pleasure or well-being. In this stage, the use of substances coexists with other sources or potential sources of well-being and begins to compete with the behaviors grounded in a person's most deeply held beliefs and values.

In stage two, the quick high or sense of well-being brought on by consuming the substance is sought *on a more regular basis*. In this stage, the individual is not yet experiencing any significant negative consequences from his or her pursuit of this behavior, and since the individual can still exercise choice regarding substance use, he or she remains faithful to his or her primary values. But that life-affirming faith is threatened by the individual's growing trust in and expectation of benefits from the chemical quick fix. It promises an easier and perhaps less ambiguous source of well-being, one that's almost instantly accessible. Despite this allure, it is still possible at this stage for the individual to discern the benefits of his or her higher values.

With stage three comes a *loss of control* over drug or alcohol use and behaviors that assault the individual's own sense of right and wrong and violate the responsibilities and obligations that he or she has in caring relationships with others. His or her compulsive use of the substance begins to create a new and harmful faith attachment that displaces previously held values, but feelings of guilt and shame accompany the abandoning of the old values. The old values were the "glue" in the individual's relationships to self and to others, and his or her embracing of those values constituted a connection to what was larger than that self and thus of greater significance. The individual can remedy the guilt that has resulted from abandoning these values in two ways: by constructing an increasingly elaborate system of denial and rationalization for his or her substance use and related behavior and by increasing his or her level of substance use to escape not only the guilt but other negative consequences of drug use as well. Typically, both of these solutions come into play.

With the transition to stage four, the primacy of the *attachment* to drugs or alcohol becomes complete. Chemicals are now the primary object of faith, the ultimate good in the individual's life, while the old, abandoned (or at least submerged) values persist as a source of profound discomfort and growing despair. The individual loses the connection to his or her true, life-affirming self and to others, the basis for which was his or her old belief system and values. Individuals at this stage are at the mercy of their false idol, and their pain can be measured in the depth of their despair and feelings of helplessness.

The attachment process that occurs in the development of full-blown addiction is as powerful as any attachment a human being is capable of. For the chemically dependent person, drugs or alcohol become the central reality of life, which increasingly spirals in on the attachment to the substance. The attachment of addiction precludes any truly ultimate commitment, let alone a commitment to self or to others. There is little room for love, whether of self, others, or a higher power. Dependent people want to love and be loved, and they will talk with the deepest longing of watching loving relationships from a distance, always out of reach. Some dependent people talk of loving their substance, but this is usually only in the beginning of the attachment. Real love is voluntary, but compulsion replaces choice for addicted people, and the chemical-dependent individual knows this is not love.

Along with physical and emotional healing, recovery means reconnecting to self, to others, and to the spirit of life. In addition, it means finding not only new, truly good objects of desire but also different ways of relating to them—ways marked by freedom of choice rather than compulsion. A healthy relationship is a voluntary one, and for the chemically dependent individual, regaining the capacity to exercise choice is a prerequisite for any hope of renewal and future well-being.

Above all, recovery is about a deep opening to life that releases the individual to love and reconnection. It means learning how to embrace both a yearning for transcendence and the pains, uncertainties, and mortality that define the human condition. It means abandoning the certainty that accompanies a chemically induced escape from our human frailties and embracing the uncertainty of living from a place of trust in love and goodness. Being in recovery means being in the freely chosen state of vulnerability.

The Recovery of Well-Being

The diagnosis and treatment of the medical problems caused by chemical dependence is usually a straightforward matter. It often begins during inpatient drug detoxification and continues on an outpatient basis under the direction of a physician. Long-term recovery, however, including psychological and social readjustment, depends on spiritual healing, indeed, a spiritual rebirth. The removal of addictive substances and substance-seeking behaviors, which have become the focus of the individual's life and the source of his or her self-definition, must be followed by a program for rediscovering healthy behaviors and core values.

Given this need, it is not surprising that historically, the most consistently effective component of all forms of addiction recovery programs has been the twelve-step self-help model developed by Alcoholics Anonymous (AA). AA's Twelve Steps of recovery comprise a spiritual approach, as laid out in the program's "Big Book":

> When, therefore, we were approached by those in whom the Problem [alcoholism] had been solved, there was nothing left for us but to pick up the simple kit of spiritual tools laid at our feet [the AA recovery program]. . . . The great fact is just this, and nothing less: That we have had deep and effective spiritual experiences which have revolutionized our whole attitude toward life, toward our fellows and toward God's universe.

These words of AA founder Bill Wilson echo the earlier thoughts of psychologist Carl Jung regarding the spiritual nature of recovery from addiction. The Big Book cites the following exchange between Jung and an alcoholic friend of Wilson, who went to Europe to consult with Jung when no treatment in the United States seemed effective in his case:

> The doctor said: "You have the mind of a chronic alcoholic. I have never seen one single case recover, where that state of mind existed to the extent that it does in you." Our friend felt as though the gates of hell had closed on him with a clang.
>
> He said to the doctor, "Is there no exception?"
>
> "Yes," replied the doctor, "there is. Exceptions to cases such as yours have been occurring since early times. Here and there, once in a while, alcoholics have had what are called vital spiritual experiences. . . . They appear to be in the nature of huge emotional displacements and rearrangements. Ideas, emotions, and attitudes which were once the guiding forces of the lives of these men are suddenly cast to one side, and a completely new set of conceptions and motives begin to dominate them."

Although researchers have been confounded in trying to explain scientifically how the AA recovery model works to maintain sobriety for many people, the program's efficacy is not surprising to those who understand the essentially spiritual nature of addiction. Meanwhile, the primacy of AA as an effective approach for establishing and maintaining a substance-free life is well established. And while it is not, unfortunately, an approach that can be embraced by everyone, its insights into the requirements for sober living should inform the thinking of pastoral caregivers trying to help chemically dependent people change their lives.

In an important sense, the Twelve Steps of AA offer guidelines for achieving wholeness and well-being that can well serve anyone, regardless of the state of his or her dependence or the power of his or her attachments. Each of us can be placed at a position along the continuum between no attachments and addiction in regard to the things that are important in our lives. One in five of us will become dependent on a chemical substance in our lifetime. Others of us move back and forth along the continuum in our relationships to substances, behaviors, people, and possessions. We achieve spiritual recovery from addiction when we learn to maintain attachments that are freely chosen and life affirming. In so doing, we avoid enshrining attachments that threaten our most deeply held values and that can obscure our inescapable need to live with both the pleasures and the uneasiness of our humanity.

Spiritual principles inform the AA program and define both the means (or tools) and ends (sobriety) of participation in twelve-step recovery work. (The Twelve Steps of AA are listed on page 122.) The first of these principles, expressed in steps one through three, is that alcoholics are powerless over their use of alcohol and that to achieve and maintain sobriety, they must accept the guidance of a power greater than themselves. Surrender, establishing a relationship with a higher power, and acknowledging personal powerlessness not only constitute the wisdom of the first three steps, but they also represent the foundation on which the rest of the twelve-step recovery program is based. As such, embracing these principles is the minimum requirement for successful participation in AA.

For many new AA members, these principles mirror the wisdom of their faith tradition, especially if they are Christian, and the theology of the first three steps is easily embraced. Unfortunately, for some people, these principles can be a barrier to participation in AA or any twelve-step program. This may be especially true for people with no experience in organized religion, those who have rejected (for whatever reason) the teachings of their faith tradition, and those of a non-Judeo-Christian background. Although there is a strong and often visible Christian influence in AA meetings and teachings, sensitive and flexible pastoral guidance can help people build their own spiritual belief systems and thereby allow them to take advantage of the unrivaled rewards of participation in a twelve-step recovery program.

The second step of AA states, "We came to believe that a power greater than ourselves could restore us to sanity." This turning to a higher power is the premise of all the activities and attitudes recommended in the ten steps that follow. But what or who is this higher power? A supreme being? God? According to the Big Book, the critical word is *power:*

> Lack of power, that was our dilemma. We had to find a power by which we could live, and it had to be a power greater than ourselves. Obviously. But where and how were we to find this power?

In the following discussion from the Big Book, it is clear that AA does not require a specific, exclusive understanding of a higher power or conformance with the religious beliefs of a single faith tradition. Individuals are encouraged to define a higher power that they find accessible and with which they can build a relationship.

If that is impossible, they need only admit the *possibility* that there is a power greater than one's self to begin "working" the program:

> Let us make haste to reassure you. We found that as soon as we were able to lay aside prejudice and express even a willingness to believe in a power greater than ourselves, we commenced to get results, even though it was impossible for any of us to fully define or comprehend that Power.

For new members who resist theological concepts and are struggling with the higher-power issue, AA old-timers often recommend using the power of the member's AA group or the AA program itself to begin building a spiritual base. Thus, it was the intention of the originators of the program that it would accommodate people of any religious persuasion as well as those with no religion at all. The program insists, however, that belief in a power outside of and larger than an individual's personal sphere of control is fundamental to achieving stable sobriety. Six of the twelve steps explicitly refer to the individual's higher power, and four of these use the word *God* with the qualifier *as we understand him*. There can be no question that the spiritual center of the AA program of recovery is an openness to belief and trust in a power greater than oneself to help deliver one from the stranglehold of addiction.

While AA literature takes pains to describe its openness to a personal definition of a higher power, as a practical matter, many people construe the program as being religious and indeed Christian. With or without qualification, *God* is mentioned frequently in the Big Book and other AA literature, and the Twelve Steps incorporate a regime of confession (namely, the disclosure of personal faults to God and another human being in step five and the making of amends in steps eight and nine) and prayer that will feel familiar to anyone with experience in a Christian church. Moreover, many AA meetings close with a recitation of the Lord's Prayer. Indeed, a typical twelve-step meeting can bear a strong resemblance to a Christian worship service, complete with opening words and a prayer or meditation, scriptural readings (from the Big Book, the Twelve Steps, etc.), expressions of faith, the confession of sins, offering repentance and atonement, a closing prayer, and even the passing of a collection basket. Most meetings are followed by a social hour, at which coffee is served. And since it is not unusual in early sobriety even for those steeped in Christian faith to have feelings of anger with or estrangement from their higher power, the life stories ("drunkalogues") of recovering people told from the podiums of AA meetings may include repeated religious references. These echoes of Christian liturgy and confession are not surprising, given the importance of AA founder Bill Wilson's conversion experience to the creation of AA and the deep influence of several Christian clergy (for example, Father Edward Dowling and Dr. Samuel M. Shoemaker) in the formulation of the Twelve Steps and other aspects of AA's recovery program.

Despite AA's commitment not to impose dogmatic requirements, for many people, these Christian trappings pose a barrier to enthusiastic and effective participation. Helping people work through their resistance to AA on these grounds may be one of the most important contributions we as pastoral caregivers can make to such people's recovery.

While many of the objections about AA being too religious focus on program specifics, the central problem for many critics is expressed in one of AA's most cherished slogans, "Let go and let God." Thus, it is not only acceptance of a higher power that is difficult or impossible for some people but also the call to surrender their will to that power. For many, difficulty with the concept of powerlessness may result from misunderstanding the first of the Twelve Steps of recovery. The first step states that the substance-dependent person is powerless over a chemical substance (or a behavior) and that it is this powerlessness that makes his or her life unmanageable. The clear implication is that by coming to terms with addiction, people can regain the ability to cope with the rest of their lives.

Loss of control and surrender, then, in the teaching of twelve-step recovery programs applies directly to drug and alcohol use, and it is in this domain that surrender is critical. In the face of repeated unsuccessful attempts to control substance use, individuals must find the power to get out from under their addiction from some source other than their own will. This said, a broad understanding of their limited ability to control other aspects of their lives is also fundamentally important, not only to achieving sobriety but to an overall sense of emotional and spiritual well-being.

In our attempts to manage the stresses in our lives, there is often tension between the coping strategies of *control* and *surrender*. Individuals who experience debilitating, unmanageable stress in their lives often seek the help of a secular psychotherapist. Their work together will typically focus on increasing personal control by improving the skills to cope with conflict or crisis. Individuals confronted by stressful life situations who believe in a higher power might be drawn to a clergyperson or other pastoral counselor to explore how their faith might be brought to bear on the situation. Their work together often employs the concept of *surrender,* the decision to let go of their frustrating and ineffectual efforts to control and direct life's circumstances. Carried to an extreme, surrender could mean giving up all agency and responsibility to the control of a higher power. More typically, however, it means *collaboration,* in which people accept the higher power as a partner in the coping process, thus retaining a measure of responsibility and agency in adapting to their difficult circumstances. Through such collaboration, individuals seek help not only in coping but also in finding meaning in crises, and the partnership provides them with spiritual sustenance throughout the ordeal. In effect, we can describe a successful coping style for someone with a relationship with a higher power as one in which surrender is used in the service of personal control.

The blending of spiritual and psychological approaches to coping begs a fundamental question: To what extent and in what circumstances can we expect to control the myriad influences on our lives along with the feelings that those circumstances produce? It is hard to imagine any life circumstance that does not reflect the influence of forces outside our control. Therefore, does it not make therapeutic sense to consider the limits of our effective control? Indeed, might not our unrealistic expectations for control beget an obsession or an addiction? Is this not precisely the environment that promotes what is popularly called *codependency,* or the excessive and unrealistic need to control the addictive behaviors of a loved one? Being preoccupied with control can itself pump up individual levels of stress and anxiety and enhance the potential for compulsive behaviors.

The lesson seems clear: In counseling people who have difficulty coping with crises, it is incumbent on pastoral caregivers to explore the limits of personal control and to consider how the distressed individual might seek resources other than personal control in order to improve coping. In this domain, psychological defenses and spiritual practices such as surrender might fruitfully join forces. Moreover, it is this sort of collaborative approach to coping that exists at the core of twelve-step recovery programs and that can inform the efforts of pastoral caregivers in providing support and guidance for recovering people in the congregation.

The central point regarding the collaborative approach in spiritual surrender and the one that can be missed in a casual reading of AA literature is this: Surrender does not require the giving up of *all* personal responsibility or action. What it does require is the construction of a new personal understanding of and relationship to control. Surrender requires a search for meaning in stressful circumstances that is beyond personal control and that can define the individual's responsibility and guide his or her actions in a new way. It essentially requires an acknowledgment of the practical limits of one's ability to exert control in the face of uncontrollable external forces.

In an interesting paradox, the spiritual imperative is for a person to be *realistic* about the extent to which he or she can expect to affect the outcome of a difficult situation. A wise understanding of this paradox is captured in the Serenity Prayer, which is often recited at twelve-step program meetings:

> God grant me the serenity to accept the things I cannot change,
> The courage to change the things I can,
> And the wisdom to know the difference.

Consider the case of Owen. After only five days in detox/rehab for his heroin addiction, he was obsessed with finding a way to get his girlfriend back. She had expressed to him that it would take her time to regain trust in him once he was clean and sober, but he wanted to change her cautious, negative feelings about him as quickly as possible. His repeated attempts to telephone her from the hospital frequently made him late for educational classes and group therapy. He was also caught sneaking out of the facility to buy her presents. He could have been discharged from the program for this infraction, but he was given one more chance. In a meeting with his counselor several weeks later, Owen talked about his increasingly desperate and frustrated attempts to change his girlfriend's feelings toward him. He was flooded with a sense of powerlessness, and with his counselor's encouragement, he prayed to his higher power:

> God, I leave it in your hands whether or not she will come back to me.
> Give me the strength to work hard on my recovery,
> that I may become a better and more trustworthy person.

With these words, Owen surrendered his attempts to control his girlfriend's feelings toward him and turned his attention to a higher good—his own recovery, with its emphasis on honesty and responsibility. His recovery was within his power, whereas immediately winning back his girlfriend was not (although his spiritual and psychological growth may very well be the circumstance that allows his girlfriend to risk trusting again). Giving up his obsession with controlling his girlfriend's feelings freed Owen to take active responsibility for his recovery, which was the primary, higher good that his obsession distracted him from.

To surrender in the spiritual sense, individuals not only change their thoughts and attitudes but also experience an expansion of self or self-transcendence. Their enlarged existence becomes rooted in a relationship with a higher good that can transform all of their values—indeed, the very foundation of their being. It is due to this sense of the transformative nature of surrender that the great world religions understand it to be more than a strategy to endure stress or to improve coping skills. Spiritual surrender accomplishes nothing less than paving the way to spiritual wholeness and well-being.

People of all religious beliefs can fully embrace the spiritual wisdom and prescriptions of twelve-step recovery if they are willing to pull back from narrow interpretations of AA literature and consider the intentions of AA's founders. According to the Big Book, "The Realm of Spirit is broad, roomy, all-inclusive; never exclusive or forbidding to those who earnestly seek. It is open, we believe, to all men." Acknowledging a power in the universe greater than ourselves and then collaborating with that power is as logical a concession as it is faithful. It signifies our recognition that the limits of our ability to understand or control all the forces that come to bear on our lives demand a commitment to transcending values for us to feel secure and capable whatever life brings. In addition, it suggests the folly of trying to be all powerful, especially in taking responsibility for the outcomes of our actions. The twelve-step literature points us toward these conclusions, which are reinforced by psychological studies that highlight the negative consequences of excessive reliance on personal control in coping with life's difficulties.

People whose personal values are threatened by the notion of spiritual surrender can be helped to understand the twelve-step program as a process, not a catalog of discrete, discontinuous activities and behaviors. Thus, the first three steps—the so-called surrender steps—recommend a starting point not only for developing a new, fulfilling, sober way of being in the world but also for building effective coping skills. These steps represent the pivotal exercise of humility, of being in the right relationship with oneself. Taking these steps requires a reassessment of our sense of self-importance and the limits of our ability to be the final arbiters of our destiny. Doing so also requires us to acknowledge the forces operating in the world that are more powerful than we are and that, despite our best intentions, can confound the outcomes of our actions.

Chemically dependent people lose all power and all agency in their own lives by persistently attempting to control their increasingly troubled lives with drugs or alcohol. Their powerlessness is a symbol of control run riot and the resulting deterioration in any ability to productively cope with life. In this sense, it may be helpful to think of addiction as a compulsive attachment to control itself. As the addicted person's efforts to exert control repeatedly prove ineffective, his or her powerlessness leads to feelings of helplessness, hopelessness, and despair.

The paradoxical underlying message of the first three steps is that chemically dependent individuals have ceded agency in their lives by forming a blind, tenacious relationship with an evil power greater than themselves. To be free—to regain choice and a measure of agency in their lives—they must surrender the illusion of total control embodied in the idolatry of their relationship with alcohol or drugs. They must exchange their false belief in the ability of drugs or alcohol to bring them happiness and satisfaction for a belief in a new, higher, and true good. And they will know that higher good because it will free them from their obsession with control. Surrender, then, is the necessary first requirement of learning a more effective way of coping with life.

The surrender steps of AA ask individuals to examine their relationship with their own personal power. Such self-examination allows chemically dependent persons to begin changing direction and to reconnect to others and to the vital life force in order to find sources of strength and guidance. Relaxing the grip of personal ego and willfulness allows AA members to attend to the wisdom of others who have achieved long-term sobriety and to the force for good in the world, which is embodied in the wisdom of the world's religions. The Judeo-Christian tradition teaches that this quiet force for good resides in the center of each of our being but that we listen past the noise of our prepossessing ego to hear it.

The first three steps of AA call for members to reconnect with, experience, and revitalize the power for good that is in them and to be open to it, to follow its lead. It is the energy in this force that will power the dependent person's new direction in life. The rest of the Twelve Steps lay out a plan of action to strengthen one's connection to this source of spiritual energy and the various forms of its expression—humility, gratitude, honesty, and service. The recovering individual isn't called to a body of religious dogma but to the universal values to which the world's religions are faithful and that are borne in the spiritual core of all human beings.

The person in recovery may follow the first three steps to instill the discipline for faith development or to lay the groundwork for a more effective pattern of coping based on a new understanding of his or her limits of personal control. Either way, doing so prepares him or her for the various activities that millions of AA members have learned are essential components of a sober, fulfilling life. These activities are described in the other nine steps—taking a personal inventory, making amends, developing a spiritual practice to maintain a relationship with and awareness of one's higher power, and serving others who are trying to get sober. They are the steps of right relationship to the self, which is where the journey to freedom from addiction begins.

Pastoral Concern for the Whole Person

If we search far enough into the histories of many cultures, we will learn that physical and spiritual health were not understood as separate entities. Healing was the province of people endowed with special powers and influence that derived from their unique connection to nature and the forces that animate it. Healers embodied their society's belief that beyond the material world, life is informed by a supernatural reality as well. Good health was recognized to require the harmonizing of forces from both realities.

With the rise of rationalism and scientific method in the West, physical health came to be associated with the mechanics of bodily systems and thus separated from the workings of mind and spirit, or nonphysical reality. The resulting biomedical model of health reflected the conviction that loss of health could be attributed to a specific causative agent that disrupted one's biological machinery. And so *health care* became grounded in the technological pursuit, discovery, and eradication of disease, and *health* was understood to mean the absence of disease-causing agents.

This focus on disease (and the increasingly complex and costly technology needed to fix our broken "machines") has created a paradox: We have studied and learned a lot about finding and removing the causes of disease, but we have studied little and thus learned little about health itself. Detoxifying the chemically dependent person's body of the offending chemical agent and treating the medical problems caused by his or her alcohol or drug use do not usually result in the restoration of what anyone would call *health*. Even with all of our medical progress, we seem to have something more like a *disease care system* than a *health care system*.

The ancient healing traditions did not focus on disease, and nor do the healing arts practiced in many cultures today (namely, those that have not embraced the Western biomedical model). In fact, the majority of people in the world are cared for by healers who embrace a radically different philosophy about how people get sick and how they heal. Like the ancient healers who brought to bear an understanding of the whole person and the natural and supernatural forces that affect one's being, practitioners of traditional Chinese medicine, Ayurveda, and Native American healing, among many others, understand that illness results from a loss of balance among the physical, emotional, social, and spiritual aspects of a human being. Disturbing any one of these aspects will throw the whole system off kilter, much like flicking one part of a mobile will set all of the parts in motion.

It follows that healing requires the restoration of the equilibrium among all of the aspects of a person's being. And interestingly, balance can be achieved in a system in which one part has been permanently changed, as when the body has become disabled in some way. According to this view, in which health and well-being derive from overall balance, biological factors cannot be the exclusive focus of healing. To healers in these ancient healing traditions, a concept of health care that does not consider the whole person but focuses on one part is meaningless.

With the aging of the population and the rise in chronic illness in the West, interest has dramatically increased in alternative healing models that attend to the interdependent aspects of well-being. The wisdom of these healing systems is leading us back to an understanding of health that encompasses more than a fascination with the detection of disease entities. Perhaps in part due to the growing interest in alternative healing modalities, conventionally trained health care professionals are now paying more attention to the biopsychosocial/spiritual model of illness.

Given the multidimensional nature of addiction, pastoral caregivers working with chemically dependent people should champion a holistic perspective on healing, even in the face of conventional medicine's reluctance to do so. Indeed, the unique pastoral opportunity is to engage the whole person—mind, body, and spirit—and to embrace a time-honored perspective on health. As pastoral caregivers, we should seek to foster balance in all parts of life; we should nurture enthusiasm for life, optimism, and adaptability to change; and we should recognize that finding hope and new meaning is the absolute minimum requirement for achieving a stable recovery and living a healthy, rewarding life. Thus, the anxieties that normally accompany recovery can be balanced by the joy and freedom that come from giving up the compulsive use of substances and renewing commitments to caring relationships with loved ones. Moreover, the discomfort of any physical consequences of chemical dependence can be balanced by a new appreciation for the simple pleasures of life that are available to individuals who are no longer numbing themselves with drugs or alcohol.

Similarly, pastoral caregivers can foster recovering individuals' overall resilience by endorsing the wisdom of such AA slogans as "One day at a time" and "Easy does it" to deal with life's ever-changing circumstances. Caregivers can help individuals examine and challenge self-defeating beliefs and clarify their perceptions of self and others. And drawing recovering people back into church life can provide them the opportunity for developing new, caring, and spiritually fulfilling relationships.

Finally, we as pastoral caregivers can offer companionship and guidance as recovering people make meaning of their new drug- or alcohol-free existence and reinvigorate their sense of self-efficacy. Optimism requires both hope, in oneself and in others, and the reconstitution of life-affirming values and expectations. Here, clearly, pastoral caregivers have much to contribute.

Life Lessons of Long-Term, Stable Recovery

If we randomly selected a thousand chemically dependent individuals, we could predict that a small number, perhaps eighty, would achieve long-term, stable recovery marked by spiritual centeredness. However, no addiction expert could have predicted which eighty they would be, nor could anybody have explained scientifically after the fact why these people were successful in their recovery efforts and others were not.

The truth is, we don't know why some people become chemically dependent, let alone why some but not others recover. But if we look at the lives and behaviors of those people who have achieved long-term recovery and who are essentially at peace with life, we will notice some common characteristics. Ten such characteristics, or *life strategies,* are common in people who are in stable, long-term recovery. And while all ten may not be present in every recovering person, they are so common in the recovering population that they should be considered compelling. Not coincidentally, these strategies also correspond to those endorsed by leading experts in stress management. Here, then, are ten guidelines that serve as important checkpoints in pastoral support of the recovery process:

- *Attend to good nutrition.* Two points are important here—achieving nutritional balance and establishing a schedule of regular meal times. Not only is the discipline of adhering to a meal schedule valuable, but the emptiness and cravings stimulated by missed meals can cause mood swings that may be a trigger for drug and alcohol use. Good nutrition in recovery also means using such stimulants as caffeine and sugar in moderation, as their physiological effects can mimic the rush and withdrawal associated with stimulant drugs.
- *Maintain a schedule of regular exercise.* The discipline that comes with regular exercise is an antidote to the loss of structure and stability that typically mark the chemically dependent individual's lifestyle. Exercise can also begin to reverse the effects of the dependent person's usually sedentary life and, perhaps most importantly, it offers a powerful relaxation tool. Sustained aerobic exercise unleashes the morphine-like brain chemicals that are responsible for the so-called runner's high, which occurs naturally.
- *Cultivate a hearty sense of humor.* There is strong evidence that laughing, like aerobic exercise, releases "feel good" endorphins in the brain. In particular, being able to laugh at ourselves helps us to maintain our objectivity and achieve a balanced perspective on life. Having such a perspective allows us to confront and deal with our problems rather than be victimized by them.

- *Be honest.* Clearly, it would seem strange to cultivate new spiritual values and not consider our commitment to openness and honesty with ourselves and with others. Beyond the abstract concepts of right and wrong, dishonesty is bad for our mental health. Telling lies makes us fugitives in the sense that we must then live in fear of being caught. Chemically dependent people are compelled to tell lies to maintain their addictive lifestyle. The torment that builds with each new lie (especially the lies people tell themselves) is a further temptation to use substances to feel better.

- *Cultivate at least one healthy, passionate interest.* We all need something to look forward to, something we count on to provide satisfaction. Passionate personal interests may center on a job, a hobby, or simply spending time with family. The object of the passion (as long as it is healthy) isn't as important as its sustained ability to bring enthusiasm to life.

- *Commit to altruistic activity.* Helping others with no expectation of personal gain can provide enormous personal satisfaction. It is no coincidence that a foundational tenet of AA is that a person's good fortunes will only continue as long as they are passed on to others. Thus, step twelve in AA calls on its members to bring the program to other alcoholics and addicts. Volunteering in a hospital, church, school, or retirement home or for a good cause can be a valuable activity for the recovering person. Altruistic activity reflects the redirection of one's focus away from the self and one's own needs and toward others and their needs. Like exercise, altruistic behavior seems to stimulate the release of endorphins in the brain—another natural high.

- *Undertake a daily prayer or meditation practice.* For individuals who embrace a particular faith tradition, this may mean personal or public devotion. For others, it may entail setting aside a quiet time for solitary meditation or contemplation. For many in AA, it takes the form of daily attention to the presence in their lives of a higher power, as they have come to define that power. However constituted, daily prayer or meditation is the bedrock of spiritual discipline in recovery.

- *Cultivate the practice of being present and fully awake to life.* The slogan "Be here now," which is similar in meaning to AA's "One day at a time" and the Latin poet's "Carpe diem," represents age-old wisdom. As such, it has become the mantra of the growing *mindfulness* movement, and instruction in the techniques of mindfulness (which have their origins in Buddhism, Taoism, and yoga) are increasingly sought out by people of every faith tradition. Writes psychologist Jon Kabat-Zinn in his book *Wherever You Go There You Are:*

Mindfulness means paying attention in a particular way: on purpose, in the present moment, and nonjudgmentally. This kind of attention nurtures greater awareness, clarity, and acceptance of present-moment reality. . . . If we are not fully present for many of those moments, we may not only miss what is most valuable in our lives but also fail to realize the richness and the depth of our possibilities for growth and transformation.

Unfortunately, many people seem to "sleepwalk" through life, a terrible mistake against which Paul warned the Romans: "Besides this, you know what time it is, how it is now the moment for you to wake from sleep" (Rom 13:11). People in recovery can't afford to go through life asleep, for two important reasons. First, if preoccupied, they are in danger of acting out of habit and reverting to substance use. Second, they are likely to miss the glimmer of new possibilities—the new, healthy, soulful reason to get up in the morning.

- *Cultivate an awareness and receptivity to the transcendent in life.* For people with a theistic faith, this awareness may be the sense that God is at work in their lives. For others, it may be the experience of music or nature, a walk on the beach at sunrise, cultivating a window box garden in the midst of the city, or caring for grandchildren. Such experiences at once go to the core of our being and seem to release our deepest love and sense of peace and fulfillment. People in long-term, stable recovery have learned how to acknowledge these experiences and make them essential parts of their lives. And through being alive to such experiences, people in the early stages of recovery begin to touch anew the true vital center of their selves. This signals a voluntary turning away from surfaces and superficiality and toward depth and fullness, an opening to the beauty, passion, even pain and anxieties of life where the soul reaches for the outstretched hand of God. While prayer or meditation can bring such an awareness, this characteristic of people in stable recovery is less a focused, time-circumscribed activity and more a way of being in the world. Being open to such experiences as we go about our lives belies the notion that there are specific times or places for the soul to be refreshed or inspired. Like children who find wonderment and delight in life's simplest encounters, recovering people must be in the world with such openness and trust that they can be fully ready for the numinous to break through at any moment. And clearly, being open to the transcendental in life requires being fully present in the moment—being here now.

- *Participate in the life of a caring community.* All the power of the transcendent in life gets played out in one's relationships with one's fellow human beings. No one heals from addiction, no one is restored to well-being in isolation. Human beings are social animals whose well-being is fostered by participating in social groups. And there is no better community in which to heal and find new meaning than a community of faith, in which members support each other's unique growth in common pursuit of the sacred. Here, we hold one another gently through births and rebirths. Here, we are bathed in the spiritual wisdom of the great teachers of our faith tradition. Here, pastors, friends, and family members can help recovering persons discern good and essential life developments from potentially disastrous ones. Perhaps the greatest threat to long-term recovery from addiction is the unwitting attachment to a new false idol, one that may seem benign compared with the evils of heroin or alcohol. For people who have learned to rely on external sources of gratification, gambling, work, sexual relationships, and even food and exercise can become pernicious attachments every bit as destructive as narcotics. Discernment in community can be lifesaving. The essential point is that spiritual healing and growth happen in community.

The life lessons learned by people in long-term, stable recovery—with their attention to body, mind, and spirit—offer an array of lenses for keeping the whole person in perspective as he or she navigates the path to renewed health and well-being. As providers of pastoral care, we can do no better than learn from those who have successfully made the voyage.

Recovery in a Faith Community

The story is told of a church building seen on a dark night. The basement, where an Alcoholics Anonymous (AA) meeting is in progress, is ablaze with lights and activity. Upstairs, the single window in the pastor's study is dimly lit. As she has done on many such evenings, the pastor is working at her desk, trying to figure out how to spread some of the spiritual fervor that is filling the basement throughout the rest of the building and into the hearts and souls of her congregation.

This little story embodies several truths. The vital interplay of joys and sorrows, of laughter and silence that enlivens the basement is that of a *community* —a fellowship of souls who share a common brokenness and whose coming together brings them strength. In the truest sense, this is a community of lay ministers, in which individuals grow spiritually by serving each other, especially the weakest among them.

The pastor in her study yearns to create a similar spirit of ministry among the members of her congregation. She knows that in the community of AA, there is no stigma about the disease of addiction or for that matter, about any other form of frailty or vulnerability. After all, we are all broken in some way, incomplete and vulnerable. That is the human condition.

The pastor would also like to see the attitude of openness, acceptance, and mutual support that permeates AA spread to her own flock. She knows that addiction is an issue of social justice as well as a health problem. People who struggle with addiction are often marginalized by society. No matter what faith tradition she serves, it will have taught her that achieving spiritual growth and wholeness is always in large part a function of developing compassion for the less fortunate, the weak, the ill, and the oppressed. She would like to see such compassion flowing in her congregation. She can think of several members of her congregation who have withdrawn from church activities because of their guilt and shame over substance abuse in their family, and she knows their isolation is not healthy or healing. None of the people in the basement are struggling with their illness alone.

The pastor smiles as she hears a burst of laughter and then a round of exuberant applause. There is clearly nothing gloomy about the meeting, nor is it secretive. It is an open AA meeting—anyone, regardless of whether he or she has a substance abuse problem, is welcome to attend. The pastor believes deeply that spiritual healing and growth should be joyous.

Sitting alone at her desk, the pastor thinks about how she would like to bring all of these qualities of a healing community into her sanctuary and religious education classrooms. She knows from both her ministry and her experience with her own family and friends that for a variety of reasons, not everyone with a drug or alcohol problem is able to participate in a twelve-step recovery program. And even those who can and do need support beyond their twelve-step meetings. They need other people and opportunities in their lives that will contribute to their spiritual healing. And especially since AA is a spiritual program, not a religious one, the pastor understands that the religious values of her faith tradition could contribute to the recovery of people who share that tradition in ways that AA never could. Indeed, bringing their recovery into an open, accepting, and supportive faith community would be a logical step—a thirteenth step, perhaps—for religious people.

As she leaves her study and closes the door on this particular evening, the pastor's heart is full of the excitement and power of a spiritual community committed to action, and her mind is bubbling with ideas on where to begin.

While community can be important for healing from any trauma or illness, it is essential to the individual struggling with substance use problems, for a number of reasons: First, it is the nature of addiction to turn people in upon themselves, to make them become self-occupied. Second, maintaining an addiction can easily become a way of life, commanding much of a person's time, attention, and commitment. It is not typically a life that is shared, other than for the convenience of the person with the drug or alcohol problem. Third, abusing drugs or alcohol is socially stigmatizing and often illegal, making the user feel both ashamed and guilty.

Recovery must involve reaching out, reconnecting with people with healthy lifestyles, and relearning how to attend to others as well as oneself.

A faith community is uniquely qualified to serve the sick and struggling newcomer. Entering that community can open the door to the healing principles taught by all of the world's great religions (for instance, compassion, forgiveness, hope) and set the individual on the path to a new, meaningful, and joyous way of life. The caring community can also support recovering people in the process of discernment as they learn to make new, healthy lifestyle choices to replace old drug- or alcohol-seeking behaviors. In the faith community, this discernment can be enriched by the values, teachings, and spiritual disciplines of a religious tradition. The moral compass of the community can provide a reference point by which recovering individuals can gauge a new direction, a new life strategy, and a new vision for health and well-being.

A caring community can also open a safe arena for recovering individuals to re-engage in social activities away from old relationships associated with drug or alcohol use. Often, one of the greatest challenges to newly recovering people is the need to abandon many of their old relationships that centered on drug or alcohol use. While no community is completely free from substance abuse, the faith community is organized around principles and values that are antithetical to those of the substance-abusing culture. As such, it can provide a place where the recovering person can be less anxious about being confronted by drug- or alcohol-abusing behavior.

If the faith community is open, accepting, and supportive of people struggling with the effects of addiction in their lives, it will provide a set of role models for sober living beyond those provided in twelve-step programs. In this environment, people in recovery can extend the opportunities for learning again to trust and to be trustworthy. Doing so beyond the twelve-step community in the larger community is paramount, since the larger community is where recovering individuals aim to live the rest of their lives. Belonging to a faith community may be even more crucial if, for some reason, a person is unable to participate in a twelve-step program. In such a case, the open, accepting, and supportive faith community can be that person's primary recovery community, teaching its spiritual values and practices and providing the social support of congregational members who may or may not have been touched by substance abuse.

For many in recovery, their twelve-step program provides a transitional healing environment in which the focus is still on drugs and alcohol, but now it's on how *not* to use them. To experience continuing growth in recovery, however, the individual must expand his or her life focus and realize new dreams and goals and meanings.

And so, even participants in AA and other such programs can discover new opportunities by belonging to a faith community. In many cases, people who have spent some time in a twelve-step recovery program look for new ways to grow spiritually. Those who feel connected to a religious tradition can enlarge, enhance, and more fully personalize their twelve-step spiritual life with the values and wisdom of their particular faith. In this sense, the faith community offers a logical extension of the spiritual groundwork laid by the twelve-step program.

The involvement of recovering individuals in the faith community can benefit both recovering and nonrecovering members of the congregation by providing rich opportunities for service to people who struggle with active drug/alcohol abuse and who are sick in mind, body, and spirit. Participants in twelve-step recovery programs are familiar with this vitally important aspect of the path to recovery—that it is just as important to one's spiritual health to care for others as it is to be cared for oneself.

By bringing its commitment to service to bear in the wider community, the faith community can spread the power of its healing. Sharing its belief in the worth and dignity of every human being and demonstrating their commitment to reduce the stigma of addiction, members of the congregation can bring hope to many users of drugs and alcohol, who are often marginalized by society. For many people, this stigma remains the single biggest barrier to seeking help. An open and accepting faith community can model its healing efforts within its own religious tradition as well as create opportunities for interfaith collaboration. Through sharing resources and building on each other's initiatives and experience, faith communities can expand the network of safe and healing places for people dealing with addiction.

Another valuable role of the faith community is to create a safety net for its children. Children should have access to a place where they can find direction and support in dealing with the drug and alcohol experimentation that is part of their lives today. The faith community can create a place of open, honest, and nonjudgmental discussion, in which young people feel safe seeking help and counsel and understand that the fundamental commitment is to protect them from the harm that drug or alcohol use can cause. This should be a place where even the most troubled child will be held closely and never abandoned.

Since both parents and children are invited into the life and activities of the faith community, it can extend the safety net and draw in the family struggling with a child's drug and alcohol issues. In addition to responding to children's needs, the faith community can provide strength and support to confused and distraught parents, many of whom have few identifiable resources to turn to as they try to shepherd their children safely through the drug and alcohol experiences of adolescence.

Individuals of all ages can benefit from examining the place of drugs and alcohol in their lives. For instance, young adults might find in an open, accepting, and supportive faith community the suitable environment to look at these issues as they make the transition from adolescence and face the commitments and responsibilities of adult life. Seniors, as well, might find the familiar environment of the faith community a safe and comfortable place in which to consider their potential for alcohol or drug abuse, which is on the rise in aging populations.

In addition, the faith community can prompt its members to examine their attitudes and biases regarding the illness of addiction. Like many forms of prejudice, misinformed and hurtful attitudes regarding drug and alcohol abuse are part of the fabric of American society. Yet the reality is that we as a society will not come to grips with this national health epidemic until more of us examine our personal beliefs regarding addiction and give up our negative stereotypes of victims of chemical dependence.

Finally, the committed faith community can contribute a new dimension to the continuum of care for people recovering from addiction, supplementing a system that is often fragmented and especially lacking in resources for family and other loved ones of these recovering individuals. An open, accepting, and supportive faith community can serve as an important recipient of referrals from health care workers in their efforts to connect recovering people with nonclinical care providers and other community support systems.

Becoming involved in the process of recovery can transform a community of faith, bringing a new sense of mission and purpose and re-energizing its members. Ideally, this transformation will create a broader awareness and acceptance of our individual vulnerability and our deep spiritual need to care for and be cared for by one another whenever we become hurt in body, mind, or spirit.

Recovery without Twelve-Step Support

While AA and other twelve-step programs have undoubtedly helped countless individuals achieve and maintain clean and sober lives, many people are able to change their destructive addictive behaviors without the help of such programs. In fact, many simply resolve to change their lives and do just that, all by themselves. One of the most difficult drugs to give up (and arguably the deadliest) is tobacco. It is the experience of many drug-dependent people that stopping smoking is harder than giving up heroin, cocaine, or alcohol. Yet most tobacco users who break their habit do so without any institutional help. The point here isn't that chemically dependent individuals should be encouraged to go it alone in their efforts to change their self-destructive behavior. Many drug-dependent people will never be able to recover without professional help because the foundations of their well-being—physical, emotional, familial, social, vocational—have been seriously eroded by their drug or alcohol use. Just as importantly, it is a lot harder for anyone to make significant lifestyle changes without support, guidance, and reinforcement from loved ones and concerned others. Such support from people who have been through a similar lifestyle change can be especially critical.

Nevertheless, people do get clean and sober without going through twelve-step programs. Since most providers of substance abuse treatment and recovery services work with the twelve-step model, individuals who choose different paths to sobriety will find fewer supportive environments within which to heal. These individuals are especially good candidates for participation in an addiction ministry program.

Developing a lay addiction ministry will involve certain organizational work, such as providing pastoral care and implementing programming and other initiatives within the congregation and in the wider community. But at its most essential, an addiction ministry is about transforming a faith community into a safe and supportive environment, in which people whose lives have been damaged by addiction can heal and grow spiritually.

The Role of the Pastoral Caregiver

One of the most important steps that a congregation can take to prepare itself to become a healing environment is to identify those members who are willing and able to take personal responsibility for ministering to people who are addicted. These pastoral caregivers comprise the *addiction ministry committee*. Whether they are ministers or laypeople, these individuals can offer a great deal in terms of spiritual guidance, compassion, support, and practical resources.

However, as a practical matter, there are only limited ways that members of the congregation who do not have professional training in psychology, medicine, or specifically addiction treatment can help an active substance abuser. Almost invariably, the abusing individual will come to the pastoral caregiver for help because of mounting problems in his or her life, often focusing on a particular crisis that needs immediate attention. While the pastoral caregiver may be able to help with the crisis at hand, he or she must always be prepared to refer the individual to a substance abuse professional if drug or alcohol use is a suspected underlying issue.

That professional can provide a thorough assessment of the full range of the individual's unique constellation of chemical dependence symptoms and related life problems. An appropriate diagnosis and treatment plan can only be formulated on the basis of such an assessment. After that, the pastoral caregiver can support and encourage the individual's compliance with an overall treatment plan and join with the individual in attending to the spiritual aspects of his or her recovery.

Above all, the pastoral counselor should recognize the danger of attempting to take on a primary role in a chemically dependent person's treatment and recovery program. Given the overlap of psychological and spiritual issues, the pastoral caregiver can easily become involved beyond his or her capabilities. For instance, active alcohol dependence can produce signs of depression, as can the confusion and fears that often accompany early recovery. But many people experience significant depression before they get involved with drugs or alcohol. Indeed, their early experimentation with these substances may represent attempts at self-medication for a persistent mood disorder. Thus, signs of depression may alone constitute a reason to refer someone for professional evaluation. Any sign of underlying mental illness should prompt a referral to a psychologist, psychiatrist, or other mental health professional.

While it is the job of professional health care providers to manage the treatment and rehabilitation of chemically dependent individuals, a faith community and its pastoral caregivers have a number of opportunities to support these individuals' healing and growth toward wholeness. For instance, considering how drug or alcohol use typically wreaks havoc in a person's life, any number of specific problems related to family, job, legal authorities, and physical and psychological health may bring him or her to a pastoral caregiver for help. Depending on whether the individual connects the crisis at hand with his or her substance abuse, it may provide an opportunity for the pastoral caregiver to address the larger problem. Typically, however, the individual's denial system is firmly in control, and he or she will not see the current crisis as a consequence of substance abuse.

Regardless, the first order of business for the pastoral caregiver should be to address the present circumstances and provide whatever counsel or support seems to be called for. If substance use is overtly a factor (for instance, the individual has been charged with driving under the influence of drugs or alcohol), it may be considered "fair game" for discussion, but only after the immediate problem has been resolved. Once that has been done, the pastoral caregiver may return to the drug or alcohol issue to explore the individual's feelings about his or her substance use, including whether and to what extent it is problematic.

If the individual seems open to such a discussion, the pastoral caregiver should make an appointment with him or her for the near future to continue talking and to consider referral to professional substance abuse help. The individual will probably resist this invitation, in which case the caregiver should at least keep the issue of drug or alcohol use on the table. Breaking through a chemically dependent person's denial system or ambiguity about the need for professional help is often possible only when the negative consequences of his or her substance use have accumulated and caused serious difficulty. Making that connection in the current crisis can be important for the individual's eventual acknowledgment of his or her problematic substance use and movement toward treatment.

Meanwhile, the focus should be on the immediate crisis. In addition to helping with that crisis, the pastoral caregiver should view the current situation as an opportunity to build rapport with the chemically dependent person and to make it easier for her or him to come forward later and get help. If the crisis involves the person's family members, the caregiver should be alerted to the likelihood that they will need help and support as well.

Chemically dependent people may approach a pastoral caregiver to get help dealing with their drug or alcohol use, but they are just as likely to want to fix the turmoil in their lives without making the connection between their problems and their substance use. When working with such a person, the pastoral caregiver can help him or her discern patterns of substance use and their consequences as well as address his or her readiness to change these self-destructive behaviors. (A brief alcohol abuse assessment tool is provided on page 123.) If the individual is still in denial, the challenge for the pastoral caregiver (or a professional substance abuse counselor) will be to help him or her move toward an acknowledgment that his or her drug or alcohol use is problematic. When the signs of problematic substance use have been established, it is time for the pastoral caregiver to refer the troubled individual to a professional in substance use disorders for a complete assessment and an investigation of treatment options.

It cannot be stressed too strongly that the pastoral caregiver should not attempt a formal diagnosis of substance use disorder. Especially in the case of an individual who has already acknowledged a drinking or drug problem, the immediate issue should be *referral*. Even in the case of suspected chemical dependence, unless the pastoral caregiver has training in stages of change counseling, helping a person come to understand the nature of his or her substance use problem is best left to a specialist.

The family or friends of a chemically dependent person may approach the pastoral caregiver for advice on mounting a formal intervention, that is, confronting him or her to force the issue of treatment. There is some disagreement in the treatment community about the effectiveness of *interventions,* and the pastoral caregiver should not hesitate to direct the family to a professional who can advise them on the subject. Many variables can affect the outcome or usefulness of such an event. At minimum, it must be carefully planned and directed, and each participant must be fully committed and well rehearsed. Most substance abuse care providers and treatment facilities can recommend intervention specialists, and family members should be directed to such experts to help them decide on the appropriateness of this approach in their circumstances.

Reintegration into the Life of the Church

An invitation to participate in the service work of the church may be the most sensitive gift that can be offered a recovering person. Re-establishing caring relationships with others—especially relationships in which the emphasis is on service—is a fundamental requirement of spiritual healing. It is not enough to be cared for in recovery; the recovering individual must have the opportunity to care for others. Such an individual might be steered toward committees or other active groups that include people who have achieved long-term, stable sobriety and who can act as role models. And once the recovering individual has achieved some stable recovery time, he or she might be encouraged to join others involved in addiction ministry work. (Note that the amount of time will vary from individual to individual, but a minimum of one year's sobriety is a useful benchmark.)

As the recovering individual grows in all the dimensions of his or her wholeness, fellow community members in long-term, stable recover can offer guidance and support using the practical approaches to spiritual healing reflected in their experience. This guidance might include encouraging the individual to periodically examine his or her deeply held values and beliefs and relationship to a higher power. It might also provide an opportunity for reflection on the spiritual aspects of his or her recovery program, be it AA or another twelve-step program. If the individual has any barriers to active and effective participation in a twelve-step program, he or she should be supported and guided in addressing and resolving these issues. Finally, the recovering individual can be introduced to or supported in the practice of such spiritual disciplines as meditation and prayer.

In all aspects of spiritual guidance, the pastoral caregiver should keep a broad, whole-person perspective and not lose sight of the importance of such issues as good nutrition, exercise, intellectual stimulation, and social engagement. Taking this view of health and wholeness is important, since many of an individual's care providers will typically focus on one narrow aspect of the person's health and well-being. Thus, the essence of the pastoral caregiver's gift is the caring presence, support, and attention to all aspects of the recovering person's life that he or she can uniquely provide.

The Addiction Ministry Committee

Regardless of whether or not a minister provides the impetus for an addiction ministry, the program presents an opportunity to develop an empowering lay ministry. A faith community's commitment to making a difference in the lives of those members touched by drug or alcohol use may be difficult to meet if it is left exclusively to an already overworked pastor. Moreover, among the many lessons we have learned during the nearly seventy years that Alcoholics Anonymous (AA) has brought its program to countless alcoholics is that extraordinary spiritual benefits flow to individuals who help others. Indeed, AA can be characterized as a worldwide lay ministry comprised of average people who, in their mutual woundedness, bring support and hope into one another's lives. This is both the purpose and the possibility for a church-based addiction ministry.

A committed pastor can play a fundamental and vital role in the establishment and growth of such a ministry in his or her church. Bringing to bear his or her pastoral caregiving skills will certainly be important. In addition, the minister can provide ongoing support, encouragement, and spiritual guidance to committee members in their work. The minister can also help ensure, as perhaps no one else can, that the addiction ministry is fully recognized and integrated into the life of the church. Thus, through the minister's interactions with various committees and lay leaders, as well as through preaching and other aspects of his or her position, he or she can convey an openness and commitment to the needs of addicted people and the value of the congregation's initiatives on their behalf. The minister can, first and foremost, promote the appropriateness of the work in the church community. Finally, the minister can use laypeople to extend his or her pastoral reach by calling on them for help in ministering to people with substance abuse problems.

From every perspective, a church-based addiction ministry should be an opportunity for lay ministry that addresses the needs of both church members and the larger community. A vital role for the minister, then, is the care and nurturing of the laypeople who take on the work of addiction ministry. These people provide pastoral care in the form of serving on an addiction ministry committee, volunteering as first responders in the event of a crisis, and organizing and leading addiction support groups. These lay pastoral caregivers are the backbone of any addiction ministry.

An addiction ministry has the potential to touch the lives of virtually every church member by promoting awareness, education, and prevention. To grow and thrive in serving the community, it needs an organizational base that can bring together all church constituencies in its planning and program development activities. To this end, a church should consider forming an *addiction ministry committee (AMC),* whose members reflect a cross-section of the church community.

Several basic guidelines may be useful in building and empowering such a committee. For instance, the core committee membership should include participants representing the ministry and the lay ministry/leadership, parents and young people, religious education program staff and youth advisors, and recovering individuals and family members. The personal characteristics most desirable in committee members include congregational membership, emotional stability, a caring and empathic personality, good active-listening skills, the ability to preserve confidentiality, and knowledge or experience with twelve-step recovery programs.

In addition, church members who are trained addiction counselors or other health care professionals and have experience working with addicted people can play an important role in the work of the addiction ministry. Among other contributions, these professionals can do training work with AMC members on the fundamentals of addiction science and the topics of prevention and treatment. Such training can be empowering and an important component of building a strong and effective committee. However, formal addiction training or experience is not as important for AMC members as the heartfelt desire to make a difference in the lives of people trying to overcome chemical dependence.

The opportunity for an effective ministry to serve people who are chemically dependent does not require providing counseling services. Indeed, any type of formal addiction counseling that goes beyond the brief assessment and referral offered by trained pastoral caregivers (such as the minister) is beyond the scope of the AMC's mission. Instead, the AMC should have resources on hand to make referrals to such providers outside the church. (An alternative scenario would be to contract with a credentialed counselor to be in residence a certain number of hours each week to assess the treatment needs of church members. This approach would be analogous to the health screenings performed by parish nurses in church-based health ministry programs, which are gaining widespread acceptance in several religious denominations. Such a position could provide a volunteer opportunity for a church member with the appropriate training.)

The AMC should compose a mission statement or other formal documentation of its philosophy and purpose. These specific principles should be reflected in that statement:

- Committee members will treat addicted people with respect, acknowledging their worth and dignity as human beings and their right to health, wholeness, and a fulfilling, productive life.
- Committee members will commit their time, caring, and nonjudgmental attention to addicted people seeking help and be prepared to listen to and partner with them even in their struggles.
- Committee members will participate in the ongoing process of assembling resources for awareness, education, prevention, and treatment referral for addicted people and their loved ones.
- Committee members will strive to reduce the stigma attached to addiction and the people it touches and to respond to affected people in ways that ease their feelings of shame and guilt.

The AMC should begin meeting twice a month and continue to do so until everyone is comfortable with the procedures and operation of the group. After that, meeting once a month will usually be enough. Early on, the committee should appoint a chairperson (perhaps serving on a six-month rotating basis) to set agendas, facilitate meetings, and represent the AMC in church governance and program groups. This latter representation is especially important, since awareness of the committee's work must be integrated into the structure and functioning of the church as a whole.

Indeed, committee members should be prepared to serve as teachers throughout the church community, making addiction awareness part of all relevant church events and activities. Self-education in addiction science, prevention, and treatment is particularly important as preparation for this role. For instance, committee members who aren't familiar with twelve-step programs should attend open local meetings of AA and other similar groups to familiarize themselves with these programs and their philosophies. Perhaps most important, the work of the AMC should be conducted such that committee members can participate from a place of caring and trust for one another.

The rest of this chapter presents an array of programs and initiatives that an AMC can launch as components of an addiction ministry in its community of faith. Some are presented briefly as ideas for exploration and development. They follow no particular order in terms of importance or sequence of implementation. Those choices and priorities should be determined according to the interests and backgrounds of ministry participants, as well as the needs of the congregation and the availability of church and community resources. As participants in the addiction ministry organize to do their work, they may find it useful to create a small list of program goals for the year, keeping in mind that some programs, once launched, will need regular attention and maintenance. The overarching goal of all programs and initiatives should be to reduce the stigma often attached to substance use disorders by increasing every church member's awareness of drug and alcohol issues, the disease of addiction, opportunities for prevention work, and the recovery needs of people in the congregation and the larger community.

Education for AMC Members

The members of the AMC should receive ongoing training in drug and alcohol issues, beginning with an overview of addiction studies and concepts, including the following:

- models of addiction (for instance, the disease or medical model, the biopsychosocial model, etc.)
- spiritual perspectives on addiction
- up-to-date information on drugs of abuse (pages 113–119 in this book provide an overview of commonly abused substances)
- theories and models of prevention
- treatment modalities and the continuum of care
- needs of special populations (such as youth, the HIV/AIDS population, individuals with disabilities, etc.)
- basics of twelve-step programs

Not only will training AMC members make them more effective in providing support and guidance to those individuals who need it, but it will also provide a special incentive for AMC members to become involved, a mark of the important work they are doing, and an opportunity for personal growth.

A drug or alcohol training workshop should be offered to members of the AMC, and it should be repeated as often as the committee has a significant number of new members. The workshop can be presented by a committee member with a background in drug or alcohol treatment and prevention, or a local professional can be invited to give the workshop.

Beyond this core training, AMC members should keep up to date on changes in local treatment services, policies, and procedures, as well as drug- and alcohol-related public policy debates and initiatives. Inviting local professionals to speak about treatment, prevention, and policy issues at committee meetings will inspire active participation in the ministry and expand the committee's capacity for responding to congregational needs.

The overall goal of AMC training is not to create a cadre of addiction counselors or treatment and prevention experts. Rather, it is to provide committee members with the background and understanding needed to be sensitive listeners in their dealings with substance-dependent people and to assist them in getting the professional help they need. Training should also motivate AMC members to build an open and affirming environment in which people touched by addiction can find spiritual nourishment.

Since a primary goal of the church's addiction ministry is to raise awareness among the staff and congregation about drug and alcohol issues, much of the AMC's time and attention will likely involve the sponsorship and development of classes, workshops, and other educational offerings. The most critical church constituencies for training include members of the AMC, the minister and other staff members, the religious education staff and volunteers, and the parents of children in the religious education program. If the church has a formal lay ministry program or in any way uses laypeople to extend the pastoral reach of the minister, they can be invited to join in the work of the AMC and in any training.

Less extensive but no less important presentations can be organized for church standing committees and other groups. These presentations should focus on drug and alcohol abuse and dependence as a major U.S. health issue, the need to eliminate the stigma attached to chemical dependence, and what churches can do to help chemically dependent individuals and their families. Everyone in the church should understand the goal of creating a safe and supportive environment in which people affected by chemical dependence can find spiritual healing.

Education for Church Staff

The AMC should offer a drug and alcohol awareness class for church staff, particularly the religious education program director, church administration personnel, and other employees who regularly come in contact with members of the congregation. If a separate workshop for the religious education staff and volunteers has not been planned, they should be invited to the staff class as well. Staff can be trained at a workshop designed for training AMC members. However, staff training is generally shorter and places greater emphasis on the role of communities of faith and the AMC's specific plans.

In any case, the content of the staff training should include these topics:

- substance abuse as the premier health issue in the United States
- facts about prevention and treatment
- what the church can do for its members and the broader community
- programs and planning initiatives offered by the AMC

In addition, a primary goal of training is to help staff members learn the following:

- to be understanding and sympathetic to church members whose lives have been touched by addiction
- to make appropriate referrals to the minister or designated AMC members when approached by someone seeking help for a drug or alcohol problem
- to be sensitive to the signs of chemical dependence issues in church members so that the minister or designated AMC members can be alerted to potential problems
- to infuse the daily work of the church with a sensitivity to drug and alcohol issues and the needs of people affected by addiction
- to understand the programs and goals of the AMC and be able to handle inquiries concerning this ministry

Education for Religious Educators

Church members who are parents, church staff and lay people who are responsible for aspects of the church's religious education program, and others who routinely come in contact with youth in the congregation should receive drug- and alcohol-awareness training. One of the advantages of organizing such training for parents, RE staff, and others is that it involves a shared approach and perspective on drug and alcohol issues, such that everyone is provided with the same factual information, vocabulary, insights, goals, and objectives.

Even if the RE curriculum incorporates a drug and alcohol component for students at all grade levels (which is very rarely the case), it should not be assumed that this teaching will address all the questions and needs of children and their parents. Nor should it be assumed that the curriculum will provide parents and teachers with the background and understanding needed to be helpful to these youth in their dealings with drugs and alcohol. Many developmental psychologists today believe that drug and alcohol experimentation is a necessary part of normal childhood and adolescent development. Given this, the first, second, and third grades are not too early to begin acknowledging the reality of drugs and alcohol in children's lives. Even if they disagree, parents and teachers should arm themselves with the facts, disabuse themselves of the myths, and understand the real dangers of experimentation with drugs and alcohol. Perhaps most importantly, parents and teachers should prepare themselves to be effective in *secondary prevention*—that is, to recognize the early signs of drug and alcohol experimentation and the danger signals that indicate that experimentation is becoming problematic.

Under the guidance of the AMC, parent and religious education staff training in childhood and adolescent drug and alcohol issues should be offered at the beginning of each church schoolyear. It may be presented by an appropriately trained AMC member, or a professional from the community may be brought in to teach the class. Either way, the content should include the following subjects at minimum:

- an overview of common drugs of abuse
- theories and models of the progression of drug and alcohol use in children
- the prevalence and patterns of drug and alcohol use among youth
- the signs and symptoms of problematic substance use
- childhood risk factors and protective factors
- parenting strategies for minimizing risk factors and enhancing protective factors
- intervention strategies appropriate for religious education staff

Ongoing Adult Education

The AMC can make available to all adult church members a drug- and alcohol-awareness class. Such a class can be offered regularly—say, twice a year or as needed based on demand and the rate of church membership growth. Whether presented by an AMC member or a substance abuse professional from the community, an adult education class should cover this basic information:

- the prevalence and patterns of drug and alcohol use
- the signs and symptoms of problematic substance use
- the basics of prevention and treatment
- the resources and services offered by the AMC (for instance, information or referral)

A primary goal of adult education should be to give people the tools they need to evaluate their own or a family member's drug or alcohol use. In order to highlight the warning signs of problematic drug or alcohol use, the class can review Jellinek's model of phases and progression of alcoholism (see page 120) and perhaps the CAGE questionnaire (see page 123). With this underlying purpose, adult education classes cannot only increase individuals' knowledge and awareness of substance use but also help them identify personal behaviors that have the potential to become habitual and even dangerous.

Informational Sessions for Committees and Other Groups

In its efforts to expand the faith community's awareness of drug and alcohol issues, the AMC can create an informational session for church committees and other church groups. This session should last about one hour, including time for questions and feedback at the end, and it should serve these purposes:

- to describe the seriousness and widespread impact of chemical dependence
- to explain the role churches can play in addressing this problem
- to provide an overview of the AMC's goals and initiatives
- to encourage collaboration with the AMC

The presentation should be tailored to the audience at hand, pointing out specific ways in which the committee's or group's work could be enhanced or expanded through heightened sensitivity to drug and alcohol issues and involvement with the mission of the AMC. For instance, in speaking to a social action or outreach committee, the presentation could highlight opportunities for doing volunteer work at homeless shelters, detox and rehab facilities, soup kitchens, and the like or getting involved in efforts to influence public policies about community treatment resources and other local issues. When collaboration seems likely or a committee shows special interest in the addiction ministry, the AMC might consider appointing a liaison to that committee to keep ideas and information flowing between the two groups. At a minimum, where collaboration isn't practical, the committee or group should be made familiar with the AMC's work and the church's commitment to serving the needs of people touched by addiction.

Presenting these informational sessions to church committees and groups is an opportunity for AMC members to spread word of the church's addiction ministry. By sharing its mission with all church constituencies, the AMC will be in a better position to foster a churchwide atmosphere of hope and healing for people affected by addiction and to be a force for improved tolerance toward and opportunities for such individuals in the wider community.

The Addiction Resource Center

Among the most important activities of the AMC is the creation of an *addiction resource center* that makes available to staff and congregation members up-to-date information about chemical dependence in all its forms along with options for prevention and treatment. At first, such a center may provide only basic information, such as meeting lists, introductory pamphlets about twelve-step programs, and telephone numbers and websites for emergency hotlines and other addiction services. This collection of information will require only a minimum of space. With time, the center may be expanded to include books, videos, and other materials in addition to the core collection of meeting lists and so forth.

The following suggestions and specifications for an addiction resource center can be adjusted according to the available space and the commitment of volunteers to organize and maintain it. However these resources are organized, making them available to the congregation should be recognized as an essential service of the church's addiction ministry.

The resource center should offer the following materials:

- pamphlets from AA, Al-Anon and Alateen, Narcotics Anonymous (NA), Cocaine Anonymous (CA), Overeaters Anonymous (OA), Secular Organizations for Sobriety (SOS), and other self-help recovery programs (these materials, which explain the organization's mission and services, are usually available from their local headquarters at a nominal cost or free of charge)
- meeting lists that identify the times and locations of the local meetings of these groups

- copies of the core literature of each organization, such as *Alcoholics Anonymous: The Story of How Many Thousands of Men and Women Have Recovered from Alcoholism* (known as the "Big Book") and *How Al-Anon Works for Family and Friends of Alcoholics*
- pamphlets, brochures, and other introductory materials from local public or private treatment services (use the local Yellow Pages, addiction treatment providers, and community hospital and social service agencies to identify these organizations and obtain materials from them)
- a loose-leaf notebook with contact information for local treatment services providers, including hospitals, outpatient clinics, social service agencies, independent drug and alcohol counselors, and psychologists with useful information such as feedback from people who have used these services
- local service and support providers for special populations in which drug and alcohol problems figure prominently, such as HIV/AIDS-related organizations, suicide prevention services, and organizations that serve troubled youth (consult the Yellow Pages and local professionals to identify these organizations and obtain materials from them)
- national organizations that provide drug and alcohol information, resources, and links to websites (see page 126)
- videos, CDs, DVDs, and other audiovisual materials on drug and alcohol awareness, prevention, and recovery that addiction ministry volunteers can use to conduct workshops and training presentations and that members of the congregation can borrow for personal viewing (a good source for such materials is the Hazelden Foundation bookstore: www.hazelden.com)
- selected titles from the commercially available literature on addiction, prevention, recovery, and self-help

The center itself must be located in an area that will provide sufficient space for these materials and perhaps some room to grow, depending on the size and content of the initial center. Much of the twelve-step and self-help introductory literature is published in pamphlet format, and a representative sampling of this literature might include twenty to forty titles. Wall-mounted or freestanding racks are best suited to displaying such materials. If these racks are unavailable, provide enough space on tables or shelves to allow individual titles to be visibly displayed. Comfortable seating should be provided, too, so that individuals can consult the materials onsite.

Another important factor to consider in setting up the addiction resource center is privacy for individuals who wish to review the center's materials but remain anonymous. While a primary aim of the addiction ministry is to provide a safe space for people touched by addiction to be open about their problems and needs, as a practical matter many people are afraid of social, vocational, or other repercussions. These concerns should be respected. At the same time, the resource center should not be located so far off the beaten path that it is difficult to find or access. The answer to this dilemma may be well-disseminated directions (including signage) to the resource center. The space should include comfortable seating so that an individual can consult the material onsite.

Another location-related concern is access for people with disabilities. Both the legal and practical issues involved in providing such access should be considered early in the planning stages of the resource center. Clearly, the goal is to make the center available to all church members.

Materials should be catalogued and marked to indicate whether a particular item can be taken for personal use (such as a pamphlet) or only borrowed (such as a book, video, etc.). Materials should also be organized in affinity sections, such as Meeting Lists, AA, Al-Anon, Families, and Youth. As much as possible, materials should be kept well organized and up to date. Pamphlets, meeting lists, and materials that can be taken for personal use will have to be replenished regularly. Items such as meeting lists and contact information should be regularly reviewed and replaced to ensure they are current.

To ensure that new materials are available on a timely basis, the resource center should submit its address and other contact information to the mailing lists of local prevention and recovery groups and ask to be placed on relevant national organizations and commercial information suppliers. They should also ask the congregation to donate books, videos, and other materials about addiction, prevention, and recovery.

To keep up with the ongoing organizational needs of the center, the AMC may wish to solicit a volunteer to have overall responsibility for the resource center's operation and maintenance. He or she should make regular reports to the AMC on the center's needs and new acquisitions. In addition, everyone who participates in the addiction ministry should be familiar with its materials so they can make appropriate recommendations to interested individuals.

AMC members should remember to tie in materials from the church's addiction resource center when it develops and presents drug and alcohol educational programs. With some forethought, the center can be stocked with materials that workshop participants will be directed to for further study, as well as self-help and treatment information. In fact, planning a workshop may provide the impetus to add new materials to the center; these materials can later be made available to all church members. After some experimentation and refinement, the AMC may wish to videotape its workshops and make the tapes available in the resource center as well.

In sum, the addiction resource center should be considered a basic service of the church's addiction ministry. The range and number of its offerings will depend on church resources, but a core collection of twelve-step recovery literature and information on emergency treatment services can be assembled and maintained at minimal cost.

First Responders

Dealing with a substance abuse problem, whether one's own or that of a loved one, can be a confusing, frightening, and lonely process. The members of a church-based addiction ministry can see to it that no one has to face that challenge alone. *First Responders* are volunteers with twelve-step experience (and a long-term, stable sobriety, if they are in recovery themselves) who are prepared to companion people as they address their addiction and embark on new lives.

A lay program of First Responders can significantly strengthen the resources of the parish minister in meeting the pastoral care needs of the congregation. Moreover, to the extent that First Responders are willing to be visible in the congregation, they can be role models of living a good life in recovery and evidence that recovery programs work. And while the calls to First Responders may be few, the very existence of such a group declares the faith community's commitment to be ready to respond to those who reach out for help.

Typically, First Responders can be of help in these ways:

- accompanying someone to his or her first twelve-step meeting or to a treatment facility
- recommending sources of information on addiction and recovery
- helping someone in recovery find resources for treatment
- sharing her or his personal experience and being a source of inspiration and hope

First Responders are limited in both the scope and the nature of their interaction with the individuals they serve. They are not meant to act as addiction counselors, twelve-step sponsors, or long-term companions. While friendships may be formed, the goal of this component of an addiction ministry is to help get people moving on their road to recovery. As their name implies, First Responders represent a starting point. There should be no expectation of a longer commitment.

Ideally, the group of First Responders will reflect the diversity of the congregation: young and old, male and female, gay and straight. Likewise, the ethnic and racial mix of the membership should be considered in seeking volunteers. Beyond these factors, individuals who are effective First Responders have these qualities:

- They are compassionate, caring individuals people who are able to interact with people in need in a nonjudgmental and confidential manner.
- They have good listening skills.
- They are knowledgeable about the twelve-step recovery process and local twelve-step meetings, including Al-Anon.
- If they are in recovery themselves, they have a long-term, stable sobriety (at least two years).

The personal addiction and recovery experience of First Responder volunteers should be augmented with drug- and alcohol-awareness training, including a review of local recovery resources, training in active listening, and any other educational experiences available locally that are suitable for someone preparing for a lay ministry with people in need. First Responders should also be familiar with the other services and resources provided by the faith community that might be of use to the people they serve.

First Responders should be supervised by the minister or someone in the addiction ministry with professional pastoral or psychological care experience. Supervision is essential to helping the volunteers maintain strong interpersonal boundaries and deal with any difficult or unusual issues that might arise in the course of their ministry. The supervisor should schedule supervision or debriefing sessions with the First Responders as a group; the frequency of such meetings will depend on their level of activity.

To help First Responders be more useful to the people they serve, each can be equipped with a kit that includes lists of local twelve-step meetings (including AA and Al-Anon, at a minimum), introductory pamphlets for the twelve-step programs present in the area, and a list of local contacts for addiction assessment and treatment, including local detox and rehab facilities and providers. These materials can be obtained and replenished as needed from the church's addiction resource center. Indeed, First Responders should advise anyone who contacts them about the variety of information available at the center.

It is important to make the First Responders program visible in the church and to let members know how to contact these volunteers. This information should be posted on church bulletin boards and published regularly in congregational communications (such as the worship service bulletin, newsletter, and website). Those volunteers who are willing to have their names and contact information published can be available for direct calls from people in need. Alternatively, all of the calls made to First Responders can go to one person for screening and then assigned to particular volunteers. The screener may be one of the First Responders (perhaps on a rotational basis), an AMC member, or the minister. As with all the work of the First Responders (and indeed, the AMC), all calls should be considered confidential.

Support Groups

Another important element in a church's addiction ministry is the creation of support groups for people whose lives have been or are at risk of being affected by drug or alcohol problems. A support group can take one of two basic forms: It can be a purely supportive meeting, which may or may not be run by a facilitator, or it can be an educational meeting facilitated by someone with knowledge about drugs and alcohol and the issues on which the particular group is focused.

For instance, an education-type support group may be attended by family members of chemically dependent people and led by someone with a background in family systems and codependency (see page 97). In such a support group, the meetings provide an opportunity not only for participants to offer encouragement and share the lessons of their personal experience but also for the leader to make suggestions and offer guidance for improving coping skills and dealing with the challenges of being in a relationship with a chemically dependent person. Since family members are often inclined to try to fix or otherwise change the behavior of their substance-dependent loved ones, the leader of a support group should keep the meeting focused on the participants and their own well-being, not on the problems of their family members.

Both pure support and education-type support groups serve as an important resource for church members affected by addiction. The constituencies within a faith community that can be well served by support groups include the family and friends of chemically dependent individuals, parents concerned with their children's behaviors involving drugs and alcohol, and people in stable recovery who wish to explore their spirituality beyond the opportunities provided in typical twelve-step recovery groups. As members of the same faith community, group participants are likely to already know one another and to share a common theological or spiritual outlook, values, and belief system.

In either form of support group, certain ground rules should be followed. Above all, participants should recognize the need for confidentiality in group discussions. The group will need to decide whether it wants to be open (and thus continue to take new participants) or closed. Issues such as maximum group size, the frequency of meetings, and meeting locations must be decided as well. (In most cases, a relatively private location is preferred to protect members' anonymity.) It's also important to determine the length of the meeting and then to stick to it. (If time is allowed for check-in and other housekeeping chores, the meeting will probably last at least 1½ hours.)

Regardless of whether the group is led by a facilitator or not, participants should be reminded to engage in supportive, not confrontational, interactions. If there is no facilitator, group members should designate someone to keep the group on track and to watch the time.

Each support group should appoint a contact person for the AMC so that the committee can be kept apprised of the group's resource needs (such as space to meet at church), openness to new participants, publicity initiatives, and any problems that might arise. Generally, the AMC should be kept aware of all support group activity so that it can both provide assistance and/or guidance and integrate it into the broader work of the addiction ministry. Depending on the group, the meetings might occasionally include guest speakers, social activities, or outings.

Despite the value of support groups, it's important to emphasize that no addiction ministry support group should be presented as an alternative to AA, Al-Anon, or another twelve-step program. Rather, support groups should be conceived of and organized as adjuncts to twelve-step programs. Indeed, in Unitarian Universalist and other liberal religious congregations, support groups may focus on topics related to spiritual or religious barriers to full participation in twelve-step recovery, such as cultivating a personal higher power or the nature of and need for spiritual surrender as a prerequisite to achieving stable recovery.

The AMC should be prepared for word of the ministry's support groups to reach the larger community and for requests from people outside the congregation to participate in these groups. Unless outside participation in some way will unduly strain the resources of the church, such requests should be granted, if members of the support group are agreeable. This is an opportunity to expand the addiction ministry into the larger community. Whatever it decides about outside participation, the AMC should have a policy and be prepared to implement it.

Congregational Needs Assessment

Completing a yearly assessment of the congregation's needs regarding substance use and abuse issues will provide the AMC with several opportunities. First, it will allow the committee to understand patterns of congregational drug and alcohol use and abuse. Second, it will help the AMC gauge church members' interest in its programming ideas and to solicit new ideas from them. Conducting such an assessment will also demonstrate the AMC's efforts to be responsive to local needs. Finally, the assessment can be a vehicle for anonymous communication from church members to the AMC on all aspects of drug and alcohol use, education, prevention, and treatment.

A sample assessment questionnaire is provided on page 124. The AMC can mail the questionnaire to members of the congregation, but the response rate from this approach is usually disappointing. For a higher rate of response, distribute the questionnaire (with pencils!) at the beginning of a worship service and allow time (five to ten minutes) during the service for members to complete it. They can then drop off the questionnaires as they leave the service. It can be particularly effective to conduct the congregational assessment during a service devoted to the subject of addiction.

When responses have been tallied and analyzed, publish the results in the church newsletter, post them on the church bulletin board or website, or announce them at a subsequent worship service. The findings of the congregational assessment may also be useful in supporting AMC requests to the church's administrators for funding and other resources.

Other AMC Initiatives

In addition to education, the resource center, First Responders, and support groups, members of the AMC have many other opportunities to shape the attitudes of their faith community toward addiction and chemically dependent people:

- The AMC can encourage, model, and support openness in the congregation about the issues that surround chemical dependence by talking about the problem in worship services, in religious education programs, and the church's print communications, all the while demonstrating empathy, compassion, and acceptance.
- AMC members can invite church members with long-term, stable recovery to make themselves and their experiences accessible to others in the congregation. If these recovering people are prepared to go public with their stories, it will demonstrate that the church can be a safe place for individuals to confront their dependence and get the help they need.
- AMC members can make themselves available as active listeners to those touched by addiction. The simple process of being able to open up to another human being about one's addiction or that of a loved one can begin the healing process.

- AMC members can invite church members with a long-term, stable recovery to reach out to others in the congregation. If these recovering people are prepared to "go public" with their stories, it will demonstrate that the church can be a safe place for individuals to confront their dependence and get the help they need.
- The AMC can use church communications vehicles (such as the newsletter, the worship service bulletins, the bulletin board, and the website) to disseminate messages of addiction awareness, prevention, and support and to keep the congregation aware of all addiction ministry initiatives.
- The AMC can organize worship services or worship service components on the subject of chemical dependence (at least one per year) to affirm the community's belief in the worth and dignity of people affected by addiction and to declare its desire as a community of faith to be available to these people as they reconstruct their lives.
- The AMC can promote the effort to integrate primary and secondary prevention materials into the church's religious education program.
- The AMC can make available to church members short-term counseling for assessment and referral for addiction services, perhaps by subsidizing them with funds from the church. A member of the congregation who is an addiction professional may offer his or her services at no charge.
- The AMC can review the church's policy about the use of alcohol on church property and at all church functions. (As a number of churches have learned to their sorrow, it is better to address this issue early on, rather than be driven to it by an alcohol-related embarrassment or tragedy.)
- The AMC can lead an exploration of opportunities to bring the church's belief in the worth and dignity of every human being into the community—for instance, by doing volunteer work at a drug rehabilitation facility, a halfway house, or a homeless shelter. This is important not only for recovering church members (in keeping with the twelfth-step admonition to pass on the benefits of experience, strength, and hope to others struggling with addiction) but also for every church member, as it very powerfully brings home the message that "they are us."
- By making connections with other churches in nearby communities around its addiction ministry, the AMC can share resources and expand the breadth and depth of its offerings to church members.
- Under the auspices of the AMC, the church can host meetings of twelve-step programs, such as AA, NA (Narcotics Anonymous), OA (Overeaters Anonymous), Al-Anon, and Alateen.

Different congregations will have different needs and different resources, so addiction ministry program ideas should be chosen with the particular congregation's qualities in mind. Whereas a large congregation might take up several projects, a smaller one might decide to focus on only one initiative at a time. For instance, in one Massachusetts community that experienced an alarmingly high number of drug- and alcohol-related teenage suicides, participants in the addiction ministry of a local congregation chose to join community efforts to build discussion forums and to improve mental health resources for area youth. Meanwhile, members of this same congregation took advantage of recovery support groups and parent drug- and alcohol-awareness programs sponsored by the addiction ministry of a neighboring church.

Realistically, no one congregation can expect to embrace all the opportunities for service that are available to its addiction ministry. However, collaboration among faith communities can yield a rich and meaningful array of prevention and support services for area residents. Such collaboration maximizes the efficient use of resources as well as reinforces the important message that effective substance abuse prevention and treatment programs are multidimensional and based in integrated community efforts.

Meanwhile, a congregation's establishment of an addiction ministry should begin by addressing the core components of such a ministry. At a minimum, an AMC should be gathered and empowered to plan and coordinate the church's addiction programming, whether the work is undertaken within the congregation or in the community. Ministers and lay leaders alike should be consulted for advice and support, and information on local prevention and treatment resources, as well as basic reference materials, should be assembled for use by the staff and members of the congregation. These activities should be seen as laying the foundation for building a church's addiction ministry.

Helping Special Populations

Chemical dependence does not discriminate. It strikes men and women, the young and the old, the rich and the poor, the educated and the uneducated, and persons from all ethnic and cultural backgrounds.

For many years, addiction professionals responded to *all* chemically dependent people with the same treatments regardless of these important differences. However, over the past several decades, we have learned, for instance, that adolescents are vulnerable to substance abuse in unique ways compared to seniors, that men and women experience addiction differently, and that the recovery needs are not the same for these groups. The research and treatment communities have begun to be more aware of these differences and can now be more focused in their choice of treatment for any given individual. Pastoral caregivers should be no less fully informed about the ways that substance abuse is reflected in different people.

Like most general discussions of addiction, ours to this point has primarily reflected the experiences of adult males. We will now examine the important differences experienced by women, young people, and seniors with substance abuse and dependence and how pastoral caregivers can best respond to their unique recovery needs.

Children and Adolescents

In one of the largest and most respected national surveys, conducted by the National Council on Alcoholism and Drug Dependence, tracking the drug and alcohol use and attitudes of American eighth-, tenth-, and twelfth-grade youth, 54 percent of eighth-graders reported drinking alcohol in the past year, 27 percent said they had gotten drunk at least once in the past year, and 13 percent said they had engaged in binge drinking in the two weeks prior to the survey. More than 8 percent of the eighth-graders admitted that they started drinking as early as sixth grade or before. The figures for marijuana use among eighth-graders are as follows: 10 percent admitted that they had used the drug, with 6 percent admitting use in the year prior to the survey; more than 2 percent had used marijuana in the sixth grade; 3 percent said they had used the drug in the month prior to the survey; and 0.2 percent reported daily use during the month prior to the survey.

These statistics illustrate two very important points. First, drug and alcohol use is a full-blown reality of life for American youth well before high school. Second, among all mood-altering substances used by children and adolescents, alcohol should be American society's greatest cause for concern. It can't be stated too strongly that despite the U.S. government's so-called war on drugs, with its emphasis on illegal substances, alcohol is by far the most powerful destroyer of lives.

Yet acting on that concern as pastoral caregivers can be difficult for two reasons: First, young people are typically more blasé about the significance of their alcohol use than they are about their use of other substances, and second, the adult world displays a confounding ambiguity about the use and effects of alcohol.

Meanwhile, the use and abuse of a variety of substances by children and adolescents is widespread and poses a significant threat to their normal development and well-being. By invigorating efforts to help children navigate the early years of drug and alcohol experimentation, we as pastoral caregivers will not only save lives but might significantly influence adult abuse of psychoactive substances as well. Joseph Califano, chairman of Columbia University's Center on Addictions and Substance Abuse, has remarked that children who get through adolescence without using drugs, alcohol, or cigarettes are almost certain never to use or abuse these substances.

Without losing sight of the primacy of alcohol abuse as a problem among youth, it is important to acknowledge growing evidence in recent years of the rise of poly-substance (or combined) abuse in young people. In a survey of members of Alcoholics Anonymous (AA) under the age of thirty, nearly 60 percent reported that they had become dependent on both alcohol and other drugs—about twice as many as in AA's overall membership. However, according to one widely credited theory, most people who become illicit drug users first used and abused alcohol. And since alcohol can be legally obtained and consumed by adults (a significant percentage of whom are themselves troubled by problematic drinking), it seems likely, even convenient, that efforts to root out substance abuse problems among youth will be aimed at pursuing illicit drugs rather than alcohol.

Despite the seriousness of substance abuse and dependence in young people, there are daunting and persistent obstacles to the creation of effective prevention, assessment, diagnosis, and treatment programs for this age group. First, researchers' approach to understanding the causes, symptoms, assessment, and treatment of substance use disorders has been largely based on adult models. Until quite recently, little attention has been paid to the specific issues and characteristics of childhood and adolescent substance use, particularly the interaction between normal growth and development and drug and alcohol experimentation. For instance, many of the treatment programs available to young people are based on the twelve-step approach of AA, which is basically a one-size-fits-all approach with no regard for a person's age, gender, or cultural identity.

Second, addiction professionals are unclear on how to distinguish among *experimentation, abuse,* and *dependence* in adolescent drug and alcohol use. What's the difference between, say, *experimental* use and *recreational* use or between *heavy* and *problem* drinking? Not only is there disagreement on the meanings of these often-used terms, but professionals don't know how to quantify them in terms of the frequency involved, the amount of substance consumed, or the consequences of use. One influential national study classifies adolescent drinking behavior on the basis of frequency and quantity. Meanwhile, the National Institute for Alcohol Abuse and Alcoholism defines *adolescent problem drinking* as being drunk six or more times a year, or experiencing negative consequences (such as legal, family, peer, academic, or behavior problems) from alcohol use two or more times a year, or both. This definition was endorsed by the American Academy of Pediatrics in 1987. Other professionals see using alcohol as a means of psychological escape as a primary criterion for establishing problematic use.

A third obstacle to the creation of effective services for youth is that even the casual use of alcohol by individuals in this age group can have severe consequences with parents, school, and community. This is true regardless of whether the youth gets intoxicated regularly or has any other physical symptoms of problematic alcohol use.

Fourth, there is serious debate among some in the research and treatment community as to whether substance abuse is a symptom rather than a cause of youthful deviant behavior. If it is a symptom, then efforts to address the behavioral issue could result in decreasing the substance abuse problem.

Finally, many of the most frequently referred to studies of substance abuse problems focus on school populations of young people. However, it is believed that many of the young people with serious drug and alcohol problems end up dropping out of school and are thus lost to these studies. This is one explanation for the small but significant drop in drug and alcohol problems reported between the tenth and twelfth grades. It is assumed that many of the most seriously affected students do not remain in school long enough to graduate or to show up in the statistics reflecting the extent of twelfth-grade drug and alcohol problems. Indeed, the rate of disapproval of heroin and cocaine use is quite high among high school seniors who are still in school.

Since all psychoactive substance use by adolescents under eighteen is illegal, some adults see all such use as deviant or problematic. But many experts now believe that substance use can be considered normal behavior in terms of the challenges faced by adolescents during their development; various forms of behavioral experimentation and risk taking help young people understand and define themselves and their individual, unique roles in life. Most young people experiment with drugs (including tobacco) and alcohol, and most do not become abusers. Even among adolescent heavy drinkers who get into trouble because of their alcohol use, their drinking problems seem to be self-limiting. Several studies have shown that having a drinking problem during adolescence is not predictive of problematic alcohol use as an adult.

These findings should not give false comfort or promote complacency in our efforts to monitor and offer guidance to young people as they navigate the challenges of development to adulthood. (Remember that alcohol is the biggest killer of teenagers.) But it is important to acknowledge our confusing and often conflicting perspectives on adolescent drug and alcohol use.

Researchers have identified a number of risk factors associated with the development of substance use problems in children and adolescents. Some emphasize certain factors and others use categories of risk as organizing principles in an attempt to understand how young people get in trouble with drugs and alcohol. However, as mentioned earlier, research on substance use disorders in youth has only recently been pursued in earnest and so is just beginning to produce results. As with the emergence of substance use problems in adults, the point to remember is that the cause of abuse and dependence in a given child can invariably be traced back to a number of influences. It is therefore a mistake to point a finger at one or even several obvious culprits in the genesis of an individual child's problems. The good news is that many of the risk factors are controllable, which suggests the need for parents, school officials, church staff, and law enforcement professionals to be aware of the many sources of risk and to know potential strategies for managing them.

The fact that a variety of factors are involved in youth's development of substance abuse problems should also make us very cautious in blaming the parents (or the school) when a particular child gets into trouble with drugs or alcohol. Good parents sometimes have drug-dependent children, and bad parents sometimes have perfectly healthy children. Thus, many people in a child's life need to take responsibility for minimizing his or her risk of substance use disorders. It is the failure of the entire community—parents, teachers, clergy, health care providers, and law enforcement officials—to come together around this issue that leads to missed opportunities both to prevent youth's drug and alcohol problems and to detect them early enough for interventions to be most successful.

Children's biggest risk factor for developing substance abuse problems is their most obvious and unavoidable characteristic: They're kids! During the relatively short duration of adolescence (roughly between the ages of twelve and nineteen), a person undergoes more significant biological, psychological, social, and emotional changes than at any other time in his or her life. For some, the stress and confusion of these years drives them to seek relief, however transient, in mood-altering substances. Their models for this behavior are the adults they know who come home after work to the relief of a drink or who use alcohol to fix some problem in their lives. Adolescents do not have to look far in the community or the media for such examples.

Developmental psychologists suggest that it is normal for adolescents to engage in risky and sometimes defiant, experimental behavior. Given this, it can be very difficult to differentiate between *drug use* and *drug abuse* in this age group. Any use of an intoxicant under the age of twenty-one is illegal, however, and therefore constitutes deviant behavior. This means that a young person who uses drugs or alcohol can get into serious trouble without ever showing signs of abuse or dependence. We must therefore be cautious about labeling a child as a "drug abuser" or as being "drug dependent," as the stigma of being so labeled may stay with the individual for life.

Another risk factor for problematic substance use is the presence of any of several mental health conditions in young people, especially conduct disorders (highly aggressive or antisocial behavior), mood disorders (such as depression and anxiety), and attention-deficit hyperactivity disorder (ADHD). However, a cause-and-effect relationship has not been established between mental health conditions and problematic drug or alcohol use. Young people who have low self-esteem and who are sensation-seekers are known to be at higher risk for substance use disorders, and in general, young people with difficult personalities seem to be more vulnerable as well. Here again, it is difficult to establish cause and effect.

Genetics can be another risk factor, as alcohol dependence tends to run in families. Studies conducted over the last fifty years clearly point to the transmission of a genetic predisposition to alcohol dependence. Indeed, the evidence suggests that the children of alcohol-dependent parents are four times more likely to become alcohol dependent than the children of parents with no history of the problem. Nonetheless, most children of dependent parents *don't* develop dependence, and some children of nondependent parents *do*. The lesson here is that familial alcohol dependence is a risk factor but only one among several. Moreover, judging from the large number of children of dependent parents who never develop a drug or alcohol problem, this influence can obviously be mitigated.

Any serious, ongoing stress in family life can result in a poor relationship between children and their parents and therefore increase children's risk for developing a problem with drugs or alcohol. The more distant the child feels from his or her parents and the less he or she is involved in family activities, the higher the risk. A family environment characterized by poor or inconsistent parental management also puts children at risk. With the divorce rate in the United States currently above 50 percent and with many (perhaps even most) parents ready to admit to lapses in the management of their children, how should these parental risk factors be interpreted? Is perfect parenting the only way to cancel out these risks? Of course not. The factors discussed here *can* increase a child's risk for chemical abuse but do not inevitably or even usually bring about that result. Young people who develop substance abuse usually have a variety of risk factors in their background. These risk factors can be ameliorated by protective factors in a child's life, however, and this should be taken into account when assessing a child's risk for developing a drug or alcohol problem.

As children move through their elementary school years, personality and temperament issues affect their adjustment to the school environment. Children who are highly active or aggressive or who have poor social and coping skills may be seen as deviant and therefore labeled as "problem" or "difficult" children. This experience can put children at increased risk for substance abuse during adolescence, depending in part on the ability of teachers and schoolmates to accept them. Finally, children who have low grades, are truant, engage in other delinquency, or drop out of school are all at higher risk for substance abuse disorders.

As children grow, the influence of peers begins to replace that of family. By the time children reach early adolescence (age ten to twelve), they have likely selected friends who have passions and social role models similar to their own. Youth who display conventional behaviors and embrace traditional social values in their relationships and activities will be less vulnerable to the development of substance abuse. On the other hand, youth who adjust poorly to school and are rejected by peers and adults may see themselves as outsiders and find both acceptance and confirmation of their self-image among other marginalized young people. Unfortunately, maintaining membership in such a group requires participating in the deviant behavior that defines it. Most likely, this sort of group will have values that directly contradict those of the family and the establishment. Wherever children connect, their first tentative movements away from their parents and their formation of peer groups in early adolescence often mark the beginning of their drug or alcohol use. As such, this movement marks children's period of greatest risk for the eventual development of drug and alcohol problems.

Although there has been considerably more research on childhood risk factors for drug and alcohol problems, certain protective factors have been identified. For instance, having a supportive, understanding family is a protective factor for children with difficult or aggressive personalities. Children with relatively easy-going personalities can usually elicit positive feedback even from chemically dependent parents, thus lowering their risk for a genetic predisposition to alcohol or drug use. Chemically dependent parents who are able to function at high levels in certain areas of their lives confer on their children relatively less risk for chemical dependence. In single-parent families, children are at relatively less risk for substance abuse if the single parent has a supportive partner. Involvement in groups that conform to social norms and traditional values (such as religious organizations) is a protective factor for youth. Likewise, parents' involvement in their children's school programs and positive parent/child communications are both protective.

It is also important to note that a child's relationship with parents and other family members is dynamic. In times of difficulty, understanding the seriousness of the issues can motivate parents to redirect the relationship, if necessary. Thus, the parents' divorce can lead to development of a newly vigorous, positive, and healing connection between a child and each parent. Understanding the relevant risk factors for youth's development of substance use disorders can provide strong incentive for a family to closely examine its health and dynamics and to make positive, risk-reducing changes.

Several models have been developed to describe a young person's typical progression in the use of drugs and alcohol, two of which will be discussed here. It is important to understand, however, that these models are theoretical constructs based on observations of large numbers of young people. It is by no means inevitable that the behavior or progression of drug use in any given youth will follow the models. Rather, the models suggest patterns of initiation and use and therefore provide useful signs of potential difficulty, allowing for possible intervention in the early stages of a child's drug or alcohol problem.

The so-called *gateway theory* suggests that children move through four substances or substance combinations sequentially in their progression toward problematic substance use. They begin with beer or wine, progress to cigarettes and hard liquor, then to marijuana, and finally to other illicit drugs. According to this theory, marijuana is the most important gateway drug to later illicit drug use. In one study, cited by Yifra Kaminer in *Adolescent Substance Abuse,* an estimated 26 percent of young people who used marijuana progressed to the use of other illicit substances, compared to only 4 percent of those who never used marijuana. In addition, the gateway theory suggests that one in four young people will move through all four stages upon reaching his or her midtwenties and that as many as two-thirds will progress through the first three stages but not become abusers of multiple substances or dependent on drugs or alcohol.

The gateway theory does not suggest that being at one stage of substance use *causes* a progression to the next stage; rather, it suggests that many young people who become drug or alcohol dependent have likely progressed through earlier and predictable stages of substance use. The fact is that while many cocaine users at one time used marijuana, most marijuana users do not become cocaine users. (Indeed, some experts believe that tobacco has a more significant gateway effect than marijuana.) Given the statistics presented earlier, parents are right to be concerned about the widespread use of marijuana among today's youth, but the consequences of marijuana use, especially in relation to alcohol use, should not be exaggerated.

Another model that's based on the idea of progressive substance use describes five stages. The first stage is the *transition* from nonuse to use, regardless of substance choice. The second stage, *continuation,* represents the experimentation phase of drug and alcohol use. In the third stage, *maintenance and progression,* the young person falls into a regular pattern of use with one category of substance. This stage is also marked by a progression from smaller to larger quantities and less powerful to more powerful forms of the substance. For instance, in this stage a heroin user might move from snorting to injecting the drug. Similarly, a marijuana user might progress from smoking whatever marijuana is readily available to seeking out the varieties with the highest percentages of active ingredients. In the fourth stage, *progression across drug classes,* the young person begins using a variety of drugs and becomes drug or alcohol dependent. The fifth stage, *regression, cessation, and relapse cycles,* represents the individual's attempts to stop using and to maintain sobriety.

Again, it's important to keep in mind that these models are essentially theories that have been developed to describe the behavior patterns observed among a large group of people—in this case, young people. As such, they state probabilities, not certainties. No model can predict a specific child's future pattern of drug use based on his or her current pattern of use. Too many other variables are involved. In assessing a particular child, a caregiver must gather information about the child, the child's family, his or her specific drug use behaviors, and any relevant risk and protective factors to determine the need for intervention and how that intervention should be formulated.

So, how can models be useful to people working with youth? First, models can help identify potential problems by demonstrating typical patterns in a child's drug or alcohol experimentation. Second, models can be useful educational and therapeutic tools in trying to help young people understand the implications of their current drug or alcohol use behavior, where that behavior may be taking them, and how they can make corrective choices.

Treatment

While drug and alcohol treatment outcomes are variable, in general, young people who receive treatment are more likely to achieve sobriety than young people who do not. As mentioned earlier, one of the obstacles to the development of treatment (or prevention) programs geared for the particular needs of youth is the pervasive influence of the AA model of addiction. Many if not most of today's front-line substance abuse counselors, both through their training and their own recovery experiences, approach treatment and recovery from the AA perspective. Although there have been recent changes, the AA model has historically not recognized variations in the illness and treatment requirements among different subsets of the substance-dependent population (such as differences due to age, gender, or ethnicity).

For these and several other reasons, too few addiction treatment specialists are trained to address the specific issues of adolescent development, and too few treatment programs are designed for youth's specific needs. Thus, while approximately

20 percent of the people in substance abuse treatment programs are under nineteen years of age, only 5 percent of all treatment programs focus on youth, according to Kaminer. In trying to place an adolescent in a detox or rehab facility, it is not unusual for a counselor to end up calling adult treatment facilities to see if they are currently treating any young people. If the answer is yes, that is where the adolescent will be sent.

Another common issue in trying to find treatment programs for youth is the high percentage of these individuals who use multiple drugs and have concurrent mental health problems, such as mood or conduct disorders. Perhaps the best advice a pastoral caregiver can give the parents of a child in need of assessment and probable treatment is to locate a child treatment specialist who can advocate for the child throughout the treatment process. Indeed, the pastoral caregiver may want to identify one or several such specialists and include them in his or her list of community resources.

Meanwhile, research has shown that certain factors regarding treatment programs for youth contribute to positive outcomes. In fact, these factors should be considered as a set of guidelines for parents or care providers weighing various programs:

- The longer a young person remains in treatment, the more positive the prognosis for his or her sobriety.
- Both family therapy and cognitive-behavioral therapy are particularly useful approaches to treating youth.
- The family's involvement in the young person's treatment increases both the likelihood that he or she will complete treatment and that his or her behavior will be acceptable during treatment.
- Treatment approaches are more successful if they focus on a youth's functioning in the family, at school, among peers, and in the community.

Although a child's treatment options may come down to the available spaces in adult treatment facilities, some treatment is better than no treatment. Again, the importance of finding a counselor or advocate who specializes in child and adolescent drug treatment cannot be too strongly recommended. Treatment planning in collaboration with such a specialist can maximize the likelihood of a positive outcome. And as with any mental health treatment, perhaps no variable is more important than the quality of the relationship between the therapist and the client. This is certainly true of the relationship between a young person and his or her primary treatment caregiver.

The Role of the Faith Community

There are significant opportunities within a faith community for the minister, church members, and staff to contribute to the healthful growth of its children. Like the home and the school, the church represents a community of concern for the well-being of its members but has a special charge to support the development of ethical and spiritual health and wholeness.

Perhaps no threat to health and wholeness can be more clearly understood as spiritual than *addiction,* which violently disrupts the individual's relationship to self, to others (especially loved ones), and to the life force. Addiction wreaks this havoc while paradoxically and tragically promising to heighten these relationships, which can be particularly fragile during adolescence. The faith community, with its ethical and spiritual values, should point the way to developing a right relationship to the self, to others, and to the divine and be prepared to be present for young people in every respect. Above all, the church should be a place of openness and honesty, where young people can speak their minds, ask their difficult and sometimes heart-breaking questions, and make their mistakes, always knowing that their place in the community will be honored and safe. The only important barrier to our engaging in this struggle is that we sometimes don't make and hold ourselves to a commitment to do so.

To address substance use in young people, faith community programs and initiatives may include any or all of the following, depending on existing needs and resources:

• The entire faith community can join in an alliance dedicated to the care, education, and support of its children regarding the use of drugs and alcohol. Thus, children, parents, adults without children, staff, and ministers will covenant to be a community of concern and compassion around this issue. Everyone should see himself or herself as part of the web of support and be prepared to contribute to both education and prevention efforts. Because of its covenantal significance, this support can be a powerful tool in minimizing the harm that drug and alcohol experimentation can bring to the community's youth. This active commitment to the church's children should be organized as an initiative of its addiction ministry, and any information about people who need help should be directed to those in the addiction ministry with the appropriate training to respond to the problem. Organizing to respond effectively to people in need is vitally important, and making a churchwide commitment to the addiction ministry is the first and most essential step.

- The addiction ministry committee (AMC) can offer classes for parents that cover three broad areas: facts about drugs and alcohol, such as their scientific and street names, how to identify them, how they are used, what effects they produce (both intoxication and withdrawal), and how to recognize when young people are using or abusing them; the risk factors for youth developing substance use problems; and parenting strategies to minimize risk factors and maximize protective factors in the family.

- Support groups can be organized for parents concerned about their children's drug or alcohol use. Two types of groups can be formed: one for concerned parents of children who have not yet shown signs of problematic drug or alcohol use and one for parents of children who are getting into trouble because of their drug or alcohol use. Both types of groups can also serve an educational purpose if they are facilitated by someone with experience in addiction prevention or treatment. The AMC can encourage families that have been forthcoming about concerns for at-risk children to join such groups and support them in their decision to do so (for instance, by providing child care during group sessions).

- The AMC and/or the minister should be prepared to assist parents of youth who are at risk or are abusing drugs or alcohol in finding professional help. Such assistance might include a preliminary evaluation by the minister (if he or she is qualified) or an AMC member of the nature and extent of the family's problems and the drug-using behavior of the child. The primary goal should be to support the parents in locating appropriate caregivers from among the range of prevention and treatment options.

- Age-appropriate lessons or modules on drug and alcohol awareness and prevention can be incorporated into the religious education curriculum and offered at least once every church schoolyear to all children from fourth grade through high school. A regular component of these modules should be sessions that both parents and children attend and where they have the opportunity to express their concerns, understandings, and expectations of one another. Parents should be familiarized with all aspects of these curriculum modules so that they can support and reinforce the learning at home. In addition, religious education staff should familiarize themselves with whatever drug- and alcohol-prevention programs the young people are being exposed to in school and try wherever possible to reinforce the important messages contained in these programs. Churches could make a difference in prevention efforts if they did nothing more than close the loop with schools and families. If a drug or alcohol curriculum module for the religious education program is acquired from a secular source, it should be adapted and presented in the context of the values and beliefs of the faith community.

- Youth may look to adults for protection and as models of appropriate behavior in many areas, but in regard to issues of drugs and alcohol, they are particularly responsive to older adolescents and young adults. Individuals who have overcome their own substance abuse problems and who are prepared to share their experiences can bring the powerful authority of personal example to interactions with church youth and make an important contribution to their own recovery as well. Such volunteers should be carefully supervised and supported in their ministry with the church's young people.

- The faith community can demonstrate its understanding of the struggles young people face with substance use by providing an open, nonjudgmental environment in which they can safely ask questions; discuss their experiences, fears, and concerns; and engage each other and adults in straight, thoughtful, unedited dialogue. Insofar as some level of drug or alcohol experimentation is considered one of the normal developmental challenges of youth, adults may have to accommodate themselves to the "gray area" between abstinence and experimentation. Demanding or expecting abstinence is a very limited strategy for addressing drug and alcohol use; instead, abstinence should be presented as the safest choice for a young person. When abstinence is the chosen strategy, that choice should be supported and encouraged. But when it is not the chosen strategy (which will be in the majority of cases), parents and others must be prepared to accept that and then try to minimize the harm that drug or alcohol use might bring.

- All religious education teachers and youth volunteers can be trained in the basics of substance use risk factors so that they are prepared to respond to young people and their families who need their help. Such training can be accomplished in one or two sessions, totaling no more than two or three hours, and should be repeated each year before the beginning of RE classes. This training should be mandatory for anyone who will be involved with the church youth on an ongoing basis.

- If the AMC has established an addiction resource center, it should offer materials that can be used by both young people and their parents, such as books, pamphlets, videos, and contact information for local prevention and treatment programs. Among the identified community resources should be the names of any local providers of treatment services specifically for children and adolescents.

- The AMC can promote the church's involvement in community drug- and alcohol-prevention programs and initiatives for its youth. As stated earlier, the prevention and treatment programs that work are multidimensional and engage children and their parents in the home, at school, and in the community.
- The church can consider setting a tobacco and alcohol use policy for all church functions and for all events on church property. Doing so makes the faith community a corporate model of responsibility regarding substance use and demonstrates a living commitment of unambiguous concern for the welfare of its youth.

Working as a body, the church can significantly contribute to the healthful growth and development of its young people and in the process learn much about how adults need to clarify their own relationships to drug and alcohol use. Such is a commitment that faith calls us to make, both for our children and for ourselves.

Women

For all its extraordinary accomplishments, modern medicine has made an unfortunate assumption until quite recently—that illness largely takes the same course in men and women. For instance, pharmaceutical research has historically been conducted using adult male subjects, and the efficacy of each new drug has been generalized to women (and children, at smaller doses). Such has been the case with substance abuse as well. Only in the past thirty years or so has the addiction treatment community paid any significant attention to the risk factors, patterns of use, and disease progression in women. Similarly, treatment approaches that are in tune with the gender-specific aspects of women's biological, psychological, and social health have only recently begun to emerge.

While much of our discussion about addiction applies broadly to people of any background, age, or gender, there are several important differences in how women and men respond to mood-altering substances. In addition, certain psychological and social realities often play a part in women's development of drug and alcohol problems. Finally, the unique physical, emotional, and social dimensions of women's substance use and abuse mean that women's treatment and recovery needs are different from those of men. There is still much to learn. Meanwhile, as pastoral caregivers, we must be sensitive to the special needs of women trying to overcome chemical dependence—needs that may not be adequately appreciated or met in other domains of care. Perhaps the central lesson for pastoral caregivers should be not to make any assumptions about a substance-abusing woman's needs based on their experience ministering to men.

Before looking at the biological, psychological, and social dimensions of substance use and abuse in women, it is useful to consider some broad differences in their experiences with drugs and alcohol compared with those of men. For instance, while men usually abuse alcohol or illegal drugs, women usually abuse prescription medications. Thus, it is estimated that there are half as many women who abuse alcohol as men, although it appears that this gap is narrowing. Interestingly, wives who use alcohol are likely to mirror the drinking patterns of their husbands, but the reverse is not true.

Because of differences in anatomy and physiology, women experience the mood-altering effects of any amount of drug or alcohol more strongly than men. Women are also less likely to be able to predict the results of their drug or alcohol use. Alcohol enters the bloodstream more quickly in women than in men, and addictive medicines such as Valium remain in a woman's system longer. As a result of her different body chemistry, a woman can reach the same level of impairment as a man on half the amount of alcohol. Similarly, in a phenomenon called *telescoping,* women develop substance abuse problems more quickly than men. Whereas they start abusing drugs or alcohol later in life than men, they experience problems at about the same age.

Chronic heavy drinking can result in obstetrical, gynecological, and sexual dysfunction, and overall, women suffer the physical consequences of prolonged heavy alcohol use earlier than men. The effects of alcohol use on a developing fetus have been known for quite some time. Using alcohol while pregnant can result in a condition called *fetal alcohol syndrome,* which is one of the most common causes of birth defects and retardation. Since it's unknown how much alcohol it takes to cause these effects, women are advised to abstain from any alcohol use throughout pregnancy.

From a psychological perspective, men and women who abuse alcohol tend to have different profiles. Women tend to exhibit a loss of self-esteem and have feelings of shame and guilt, while men are more likely to become antisocial and aggressive. Women are also more likely than men to have a second mental health condition concurrent with their alcohol use. In fact, approximately 17 percent of women who abuse alcohol also have major depression, compared to just 5 percent of men, according to Joyce Lowinson et al. in *Substance Abuse.*

Another trait shared by many women with chemical dependence is a history of physical or sexual abuse. Women who have been abused are three times more likely than other women to abuse alcohol and four times more likely to abuse drugs. Moreover, women who abuse alcohol are roughly three times more likely to have been abused (in the past, in their present living circumstances, or both) than women who don't abuse alcohol. In treatment facilities, this pattern is so often encountered that some care providers routinely assume that a woman has been abused until they can prove or disprove this assumption.

Unfortunately, being an abuser of drugs or alcohol itself increases the likelihood that a woman will be the victim of violent crime. Women who are alcohol dependent are twice as likely to be victimized as alcohol-dependent men. An intoxicated rape victim may even be blamed for her assault, while an intoxicated male perpetrator may be forgiven.

Women are further stigmatized by the persistent belief of some members of society that addiction is a moral issue. While men and women are both likely to be condemned for their illness, women are often held in greater disdain. Similarly, alcohol abuse in women is seen to go hand in hand with sexual promiscuity, a claim for which there is no scientific evidence. Yet in one large poll cited by Lowinson, 60 percent of the women interviewed reported at least one experience in which an intoxicated male companion became sexually aggressive. In the same vein, when a father is discovered to have a substance abuse problem, he is likely to be chastised, but a mother with the same problem will often find herself reviled. Indeed, a mother's chronic substance abuse in some legal jurisdictions constitutes child neglect.

This circumstance produces a cruel irony: For a mother, seeking treatment may mean losing her children whereas continuing to drink may not. The fact is that an alcohol-dependent mother risks immediate removal of her children even if she is high functioning, has a good support system, and is seeking help for her problem. Certainly, there are cases in which the children must be removed to a safe and healthy environment until their mother has reached stable recovery. But the risk of losing their children, with their eventual return an uncertainty, is a barrier to many women who might otherwise seek treatment. The pastoral caregiver must be sensitive to the strength of the mother/child bond, the power of a mother's will to keep her children with her, and the fact that she may be surrounded by people in and out of authority who threaten both of these emotional needs. Even when separation is necessary, losing her children causes a mother emotional and spiritual trauma.

Many women with substance abuse problems have internalized the social stereotypes about the pristine nature of the good woman and can stigmatize themselves without help from anyone else. Full of shame and guilt, alcohol-dependent women tend to drink alone at home, so family and friends often don't detect the problem until it is well advanced. Primary health care providers, who are typically not successful at discovering chemical dependence in any of their patients, rarely look for the problem in women, especially if the women are well dressed, have a good education and income, and have private health insurance. Due to the prejudice toward women's substance abuse that is manifested in the American health care system, women are often treated for the consequences of undetected substance abuse with medications such as sedatives and tranquilizers, which are highly addictive.

When women finally do seek treatment, it is usually due to family or health problems. Men, on the other hand, more often seek treatment when they encounter legal or job problems. As already mentioned, the husbands of women who develop substance abuse problems often have their own substance problems, and pastoral caregivers should keep this in mind. Thought should be given, as well, to the welfare of any children at home with the father and to the risks that may confront a vulnerable woman in early sobriety upon returning to such an environment.

Treatment

Not surprisingly, certain characteristics are common to treatment programs that have proven successful with women who abuse drugs or alcohol. Pastoral caregivers and others should consider the following qualities of gender-sensitive programs when evaluating and comparing programs:

- The treatment personnel are sensitive to the special stigma (and the attendant shame and guilt) that women often experience.
- Female care providers are well represented on the facility's staff.
- Clinical staff are sensitive to the likelihood that a woman who abuses drugs and alcohol has been abused sometime in her life. Female clients can request female counselors.
- Educational components of the treatment program cover alcohol use in pregnancy, birth control issues, and assertiveness and parenting skills training.
- The program incorporates couples and family therapy components or can refer family members to such help.
- There is no evidence that women are sexually stereotyped. The program honors each woman's individuality and her unique needs and goals.
- For women who have been stereotyped or stigmatized because they belong to a racial or ethnic minority or are lesbian, bisexual, or transgendered, the program provides treatment with respect and understanding of the many life challenges they face. Pastoral caregivers may find it helpful to seek the advice of social workers and other professionals who work with these minority groups and may have experience with appropriate treatment venues.

The Role of the Faith Community

The faith community's efforts to support women in overcoming substance abuse should be rooted in an awareness of women's special needs in addressing their illness. Sadly, women in treatment rarely experience genuine sensitivity to their particular vulnerabilities, especially the heavy stigma that chemical dependence often confers. Receiving such sensitivity is itself healing. More specifically, the faith community can consider the following programs and initiatives in providing care for women addressing their use or abuse of drugs or alcohol:

- The AMC can organize a weekly support group for women in recovery. As mentioned already, a church support group for people with substance abuse problems should never be presented as an alternative to participation in a twelve-step recovery program. However, participating in support groups can be an important adjunct to such programs, especially for women, who are typically under-represented at twelve-step meetings. Women in early recovery should be told that twelve-step meetings open only to women can be found in many larger communities. In a church support group, women can help each another face the particular challenges of being a woman in recovery, especially in their roles as wives or partners and mothers. Women in the congregation with a long-term, stable recovery from substance abuse might be willing to participate in such a support group, serving both as mentors and models of recovery.
- Members of the AMC and other individuals who volunteer to help their fellow congregants through times of illness and loss can be enlisted to support women in recovery. Women who are single parents, in particular, may need this support, as the demands of treatment and recovery schedules, as well as any loss of income, may make it nearly impossible to manage alone at home. Volunteers can help with household chores, child care, meals, and chauffeuring children to school and other activities. Any church event that might be attended by women in recovery (certainly, the women's support group) should provide onsite child care.
- All congregational initiatives, workshops, and adult and youth educational curricula that focus on addiction should include a woman's perspective, especially regarding their risk factors, the biological effects of substance use, and special needs in treatment and recovery. Even programming for youth should address women's substance abuse issues so that boys can learn to appreciate girls' special vulnerabilities regarding drug and alcohol use and so that girls can learn how to be appropriately cautious in any drug or alcohol experimentation.

- Women of any age who have a long and stable recovery (including Al-Anon members who have dealt with substance abuse in their families) should be asked to join the AMC or the First Responders or to participate in any way they can in the church's commitment to women with drug and alcohol problems. Women's participation in the AMC is particularly important if the professional ministry in the faith community is male. While male pastoral caregivers can certainly minister to female church members, a woman starting out on her path to recovery may feel more comfortable being companioned by another woman, especially if her history includes abuse.

- Pastoral caregivers should be attentive to women in families and relationships in which the husband or partner is known to have a substance abuse problem. Not only are such women at high risk for developing their own drug and alcohol problems, but they may also be struggling with many difficult family issues, including parenting and financial problems. The AMC can make it known in the congregation that discreet and confidential help is available for such women, should they choose to reach out.

- The addiction resource center should provide resources for women, including gender-sensitive drug and alcohol education that covers risk factors and harm reduction strategies. The AMC can compile a list of local twelve-step meetings that are restricted to women along with a list of other treatment and recovery programs and providers. Because of the potential for women's substance abuse to cause other physical and mental health problems, such a list should include the names of local programs and providers who specialize in women's health issues. And given that physical or sexual abuse is often an issue for women with drug and alcohol problems, information about local programs for abused women should be provided as well.

- Since women-only twelve-step meetings are often found only in large communities, recovering women in the faith community can consider starting such a group to be hosted by the church. The interested women should contact the local AA or other twelve-step program service office or the central service office in the nearest large city. Starting an official twelve-step meeting is not difficult, and having the church host a special women's meeting would offer an important gift to the larger community.

- Pastoral caregivers can prepare themselves to respond to women's difficulties by becoming familiar with the surrender and powerlessness components of twelve-step teaching. For many women, the loss of power over one or more aspects of their lives is central to their struggle with drugs or alcohol. The twelve-step insistence on surrender and its emphasis on the drug or alcohol abuser's power-lessness may therefore seem contrary to their most basic recovery needs. Pastoral caregivers can be especially helpful to women by paying attention to their issues and by helping them gain a new perspective on control that will allow their twelve-step participation. These same issues may be addressed in a women's support group, especially if the discussion can be mediated by a member of the AMC who has prepared herself for this role.

- For many mothers trying to overcome a substance use problem, their overriding concern is how their illness and recovery will affect their relationship with their children. Pastoral caregivers must always be sensitive to this concern (even if it goes unspoken) and avoid doing anything through their ministry that might present a threat to the mother/child relationship. In some instances, it may be in the children's best interest to be separated from their mother for a time, but this is not a pastoral caregiver's decision. Moreover, separation from her children does not change a mother's need to stay connected with them. In most such cases, the mother is reunited with her children once she is in stable recovery. The pastoral caregiver can reassure the mother of this likelihood and support the recovery efforts that will make reunion a reality.

Given the stigma of addiction that rests so heavily on women, it is especially important for the faith community's addiction ministry to attract the participation of women, especially those who have achieved their own stable, long-term recovery from addiction. Until such participation is visible in the congregation, women with substance abuse problems may be reluctant to seek help.

The Elderly

For many in American society, advancing to old age brings new opportunities for personal growth, fulfillment, and happiness—opportunities that only present themselves when the challenges of career building and raising a family have passed. These opportunities can be marred, however, by physical illness and decline, and no health problem is potentially more devastating, especially to older people, than substance abuse and dependence. Statistically, the risk of substance dependence declines with age, but it is still a major cause of debilitation and early death in the elderly. Pastoral caregivers should therefore be vigilant for signs and symptoms of substance abuse and dependence in older members of the congregation and be prepared to respond to their needs.

All forms of addictive substances—alcohol, tobacco, illicit drugs, prescription and over-the-counter medications—are used and abused by the elderly. For instance, the abuse of prescription medications among residents of nursing homes and rehab hospitals is a growing concern. But as in the general population, alcohol is by far the most common substance of abuse among the elderly. Whatever the substance, the negative effects are similar and sadly predictable.

Statistics for the prevalence of alcohol problems in Americans over the age of 65 vary widely and are based on only a few well-conducted studies. Nonetheless, Nada Estes and M. Edith Heinemann write in *Alcoholism* that between 2 and 10 percent of the elderly population abuse alcohol. The percentage of abusers in the elderly population rises dramatically (to as high as 44 percent) among those who are widowed or who are inpatients in medical or psychiatric facilities. The percentage is even higher among nursing home residents, although illicit and prescription drug abuse is the larger problem because of the difficulty of obtaining and hiding alcohol in such facilities.

It's important to recognize that the approximately 12.5 million people who now make up the oldest segment of American society grew up when the Temperance movement was a cultural reality for many. As the makeup of the elderly population changes, the current rate of alcohol dependence among them may change as well. Some researchers believe that as the baby boomers grow into old age, their often more relaxed, liberal attitude toward the use of alcohol and other drugs (both licit and illicit) will raise the percentage of chemically dependent elders well beyond today's rate.

How older people use and abuse alcohol and their potential for rehabilitation (if they develop a problem) seem determined largely by the age at which they start experiencing drinking problems. Those who develop such problems early in life are classified as the *early-onset group*. They represent approximately two-thirds of all elderly people who are alcohol dependent. By the time the people in this group reach old age, they usually have developed many serious health problems (physical, psychological, and social) due to alcohol abuse. Individuals in this category are sometimes referred to as *survivors*.

The remaining one-third of alcohol-dependent elders are classified as the *late-onset group*. They usually have no history of problems with alcohol but turn to drinking when they experience certain life events associated with aging, such as isolation, depression, and failing health. Late-onset individuals are statistically more likely to be women, and predictably, the health consequences of their alcohol abuse tend to be less serious than those of the early-onset group.

In contrast to young chemically dependent drinkers, the elderly tend to drink less at each sitting but to drink daily. And while the older dependent person's alcohol consumption may diminish over time, this tendency should not be misinterpreted. Aging produces a progressively heightened sensitivity to the effects of alcohol and drugs (prescription and over-the-counter) due to several biological changes.

For instance, brain cells are lost as a normal consequence of aging, which means the same amount of alcohol has a greater effect on the smaller brain of an elderly person than on the larger brain of a younger person. The human body also loses water volume with age, which means the concentration of alcohol delivered to the central nervous system increases as a person gets older. In addition, the body's metabolism, especially the functioning of the liver, becomes less efficient with age, which causes a higher concentration of alcohol in the blood. Thus, in a comparison of young and elderly drinkers of the same weight who have consumed the same amount of alcohol, the elderly drinker will show a higher blood-alcohol content.

Alcohol is a central nervous system depressant, and when it is introduced into the already slower reacting nervous system of an elderly person, the potential consequences can be very serious. Memory loss, blackouts, dizziness, disorientation, confusion, and difficulties in decision making are all common effects of elders' alcohol use. Considering that some of these problems are often attributed to the aging process, the possibility of alcohol abuse may be overlooked. While aging may bring a decline in certain physical and mental capacities, it is not synonymous with the development of illness.

Having a more fragile biological system and being susceptible to a higher blood-alcohol concentration with fewer and fewer drinks can lead to numerous health problems among the elderly. The serious physical illnesses that result from decades of alcohol abuse include liver disease and brain and neuromuscular damage. Paradoxically, one of the signs of long-term dependence can be a loss of tolerance, such that the elderly drinker may need only one or two drinks to become intoxicated. This results when the liver, damaged by years of heavy alcohol use, can no longer efficiently remove alcohol from the system.

Among members of the early-onset group, the signs and symptoms of alcohol dependence are readily apparent and much the same as those found in the general population. In addition to the obvious signs of intoxication, other common signs and symptoms include changes in tolerance (the need for more alcohol to achieve the same level of intoxication), physical dependence (the presence of withdrawal symptoms when alcohol use is stopped), blackouts, accidents, and social and financial problems. Early-onset drinkers who survive into seniority almost always exhibit one or more of the serious physical illnesses associated with prolonged use, such as liver disease and brain and neuromuscular damage.

Individuals in the late-onset group may not display any of the typical signs or symptoms of dependence, which can make it difficult to determine whether they have a problem. This may be especially true for elderly people who spend much of their time alone, in which case there will be few if any witnesses to their alcohol abuse and its consequences. Sometimes, such signs as repeated falls and other accidents, noticeable instances of mental confusion when there has been no diagnosis of mental illness, and even self-reported increases in alcohol intake might be the only clues to a growing substance abuse problem.

The important lesson here for pastoral caregivers is that the biological system of an older person is more vulnerable to the toxic effects of alcohol (and drugs, both licit and illicit). Thus, certain health problems among the elderly may be the result of alcohol abuse and not the normal effects of aging. All such issues should be considered when a pastoral caregiver suspects that an elderly person may have a drinking problem.

Many of the same genetic, psychological, and social factors that are believed to predispose younger people to alcohol dependence also seem to put elderly people at risk. But the psychological and social pressures of aging may play the primary role in the development of alcohol dependence in elderly individuals. Perhaps the two most important general indicators that an elderly person is at high risk for late-onset alcohol abuse are the absence of meaningful interests or activities and infrequent contact with other caring people.

Elderly people who have lost a spouse or miss the daily routine and structure of a job may become depressed and turn to drinking to anesthetize their feelings of grief and meaninglessness. Indeed, the depression often brought on by such circumstances can itself become a trigger for excessive drinking. Similarly, social isolation, boredom, unfulfilled expectations for retirement, and the self-perception of physical deterioration (whether real or imagined) can all be contributing factors in the development of alcohol dependence in the elderly. Being alone also means that the elderly person's use of drugs or alcohol to assuage physical, emotional, or spiritual pain may go unnoticed and therefore unaddressed. It is for this reason, among others, that regular social contact for the elderly in senior centers, church groups, and other settings is so important.

Compounding the problem, psychoactive medications that are sometimes taken to relieve the symptoms of depression and other mood disorders may make drinking even a small amount of alcohol dangerously intoxicating. The same is true of narcotic pain medications and other prescribed drugs.

The pastoral caregiver should be alert for signs of any of these risk factors. If he or she suspects an elderly person is abusing alcohol, the caregiver should ask the person about his or her use of alcohol as well as use of prescription medications (looking especially for use of tranquilizers, sedatives, sleeping aids, and narcotic pain relievers—any of which can intensify the effects of alcohol). Regarding alcohol use, it's important to determine the elder's frequency of use, the amount consumed (especially if it has increased), and the context in which his or her drinking usually occurs. (Drinking primarily in isolation, rather than in social situations, is considered an important sign of compulsive or problem alcohol use.)

If the pastoral caregiver suspects that an elderly person is abusing alcohol, he or she should voice concern to the person as well as passed on to one or more of the elder's family members and friends. The pastoral caregiver, family members, and others who see the individual regularly should monitor his or her behavior routinely. If the elderly person is in a nursing home or other care facility, the suspicion of alcohol abuse should be shared with a staff member or resident health care professional who can arrange for an assessment.

The CHARM questionnaire is a simple assessment tool for identifying alcohol dependence, as well as prescription medication abuse, in the elderly. This acronym represents the key elements in five interview questions that can help indicate problem substance use:

- Are you trying to *C*ut down on your alcohol use?
- *H*ow do you use alcohol?
- Has *A*nyone said he or she is concerned about your alcohol use?
- Do you use alcohol for *R*elief?
- Do you ever use *M*ore than you intend to?

This questionnaire can be a very useful tool for the pastoral caregiver in helping an elderly person determine whether to be concerned with his or her drinking. Moreover, asking these questions and discussing the answers in the comfortable setting of an addiction ministry can be a nonthreatening and noninvasive means of addressing what might be a lingering problem.

Treatment

The options available to the elderly for treatment of alcohol dependence are similar to those available to any adult, although the selection of treatment is often driven by age-related factors. An inpatient detoxification program may be the best course for the elderly individual who has another illness, general weakness, or heightened susceptibility to the dangers of detoxification. Even after detox, inpatient treatment is likely the best course for someone with other complicating health issues. Poor nutrition, for instance, should suggest inpatient care.

The social and emotional needs of the elderly should also be considered in determining treatment. Inpatient care is strongly recommended for someone who is living alone or otherwise lacks social or community support.

The Role of the Faith Community

The faith community can undertake a number of initiatives to serve its elderly members, both in terms of substance abuse prevention and recovery support. Efforts targeting the isolation and loss of meaningful activity or engagement with life prevalent among the elderly can minimize these risk factors. One of the most important things the faith community can do is to establish a plan to be in regular communication with all of its elderly members, especially those who are housebound or institutionalized or tend to be isolated. One such strategy is a *buddy system,* in which a younger church member is paired with an elderly one and responsible for making weekly contact, either with a telephone call or a visit. As an adjunct to such outreach, many faith communities have found that visits from volunteer members of the church's youth group can be especially meaningful to elderly individuals who have lost family and have no young people in their lives. Adult outreach volunteers should attend a training session about the needs of the elderly, perhaps run by a church member who is a social worker or psychologist, and be instructed to look for any obvious, unaddressed health issues, including possible drug or alcohol abuse. If the volunteer suspects such a problem, he or she will tell the minister or a member of the addiction ministry, who can take the next steps in evaluating the situation and assisting the elderly person in getting help.

The faith community, through its pastoral caregivers, can also establish nonjudgmental, respectful, caring relationships with older members of the congregation who have developed a substance use problem, regardless of whether they have sought treatment. While the stigma historically associated with substance abuse seems to be waning, many in our society still blame chemically dependent people for their illness. A pastoral caregiver may be the first person the elderly substance abuser has encountered who isn't judgmental and who doesn't find him or her seriously wanting in character or soul. (This may be especially true of an early-onset drinker.)

Depending on how long the elderly individual has abused alcohol, he or she has invariably become isolated from others. As noted earlier, isolation is often a contributing factor to the elder's chemical dependence, and his or her behavior while using drugs or alcohol has probably alienated loved ones. The journey back to wholeness and health requires meaningful reconnection to others.

A third reason for developing a caring relationship with the elderly dependent individual has to do with hope. An elderly person who has perhaps lost his or her spouse and other close family members and friends may not expect ever to be cared for again. In order to recover from chemical dependence, he or she must believe that someone does care and is willing to help. Remember, a hallmark of addiction is the growing belief on the part of the addict that he or she can no longer change the situation—that it is hopeless and escape is impossible.

Finally, chemically dependent behavior virtually always produces feelings of guilt and shame. For a religious person, this may involve feelings of estrangement from God. Such a consequence of chemical dependence may be especially powerful in the religious elderly, who are at a stage in life when their relationship to God is of singular importance. The torment and desperation of looking at death and feeling uncared for and unaccompanied by God could be a powerful incentive to keep drinking. Pastoral caregivers can bring God's message of forgiveness and healing to these individuals and set them on the road to recovery.

Caregivers can perform a similar mission with non-Christian elders by encouraging them to pursue a new focus and purpose for their lives to replace the connection to their substance of abuse. That new focus may be a devotion to family, a commitment to altruistic activity, a love for and commitment to nature and the environment, or another meaningful activity. To be sure, dependent individuals will seek a replacement for their substance of abuse. The question is whether that replacement will be hurtful or healthful and spiritual.

The church's addiction ministry should develop a referral list of local outpatient treatment programs and counselors that have special expertise in treating substance abuse problems in the elderly. Pastoral caregivers may want to inspect these facilities, meet their staff, and learn more about their services and referral processes. The telephone number of the local AA central office should also be readily available, as these offices usually have a brief phone counseling and triage service that can give directions to the most convenient AA meeting in the area. The AA workers who monitor these phone services will also know of any meetings in the area that are popular with the elderly, who often prefer small meetings with low noise levels. If the dependent individual is confined to a nursing home or similar facility and there are other alcohol or drug abusers in the same facility, the pastoral caregiver might speak to an administrator of the facility about arranging to have an AA meeting held weekly on the premises.

Simply being introduced to AA or another twelve-step meeting is not enough. Elderly individuals who are attempting to overcome their substance abuse must be supported in their use of these programs. Elders may have difficulty getting to meetings, for instance. In response to this need, the church's addiction ministry might find several recovering people (preferably older people with long-term sobriety) who can be called on for help, either finding rides for elders to AA meetings or accompanying them to their first few meetings. These volunteers might also usefully share their own recovery experience in AA.

The pastoral caregiver can be a facilitator or go-between for the elderly person and his or her family, friends, medical personnel, and others. The caregiver's efforts cannot replace the need for a recovering individual to repair his or her relationships with family and friends (when he or she is ready), but knowing that his or her loved ones have the caregiver's attention will be reassuring and perhaps make it easier to focus on recovery. Moreover, the family themselves may need pastoring and perhaps a referral to Al-Anon.

Finally, pastoral caregivers can facilitate an embracing, loving welcome back into the faith community for returning elderly people in recovery (and for new members as well). People who are returning to the community should be encouraged and supported as they reintegrate themselves into the life of the church. For instance, their participation on appropriate lay committees and in other volunteer church activities should be welcomed and appreciated. As stated elsewhere, there is no better place to heal from chemical dependence and to seek inspiration for a new life focus than in a faith community.

The faith community's access to the elderly, whether in a congregation or a nursing home, can provide unique opportunities to intervene when these individuals demonstrate behaviors that suggest they may be at risk for substance dependence or display the signs and symptoms of dependence. Because the elderly are often more isolated than younger individuals, pastoral caregivers are in a singular position to identify the problem and offer counsel and direction in getting help.

Helping the Family and Friends

One of the most unfortunate and destructive aspects of the illness of addiction is that it harms not just the chemically dependent individual but his or her loved ones as well. The addiction of a single family member can spread its harmful effects like a virus, eventually infecting the lives of every family member. And since experience in the church setting has shown that pastoral caregivers are more likely to be consulted by a family member than by the chemically dependent person, it is vital that caregivers understand the family dynamics of chemical dependence and be prepared to respond to people whose lives have been affected by it. The good news is that pastoral caregivers can do a great deal to help family members and other loved ones recover their own health and well-being.

The facts of how chemical dependence affects family members are easier to convey than the experience of living with a dependent individual. Perhaps the best way to convey that experience is through an illustration. The case studies that follow briefly recount the stories of two families whose lives have been affected by addiction. These stories are composites based on hundreds of similar, heartrending histories shared in counseling sessions over many years. And so while they may not be real, they are true.

If your family has experienced the chemical dependence of one of its members, you will probably identify with the people described. And if your family has been blessedly unaffected by addiction, imagine yourself as a member of one of these families and hear their stories with your heart as well as your mind.

Case Study 1: John, Evelyn, and Mary

When John and Evelyn, both in their early seventies, enter the counselor's office, they are clearly distraught. During the 1½-hour conversation that follows, John, who does most of the talking, exhibits a range of emotions—anger, fear, frustration, and sadness—and Evelyn, occasionally nodding to corroborate a point John has made, weeps quietly. They have come to counseling because this morning at 5 A.M., they were awakened by a call from the police to tell them that Mary, their forty-one-year-old alcoholic daughter, had just been observed sleeping or passed out in her car, which was ensnared in a chain-link fence behind a convenience store. The police had wanted to give John and Evelyn the opportunity to fetch their daughter, rather than take her into custody. John went and got Mary, finding her awake but clearly drunk when he arrived at the scene.

John's first question to the counselor is whether he should hide Mary's car (which he bought and pays the insurance for) so she cannot drive and risk killing herself or somebody else. Many questions follow, punctuating a story of twenty-five years of ineffective attempts to change their daughter's self-destructive behaviors.

Five years ago, when John retired from his job working for the state, he and Evelyn moved to coastal New England and set out to live on a modest pension and Social Security. By budgeting carefully, they had expected to be able to live comfortably and indulge their love of exploring the Northeast in their camper. They also had plans to visit their other two daughters and their families from time to time.

But John and Evelyn's retirement has become a nightmare of crises with Mary, who has had periods of sobriety in the past but whose life has been steadily unraveling for the past several years. She has invariably turned to her parents to rescue her, often from medical, legal, and financial crises stemming from her out-of-control drinking. They have spent thousands of dollars from their retirement funds on legal bills and numerous inpatient and outpatient treatment programs and occasionally to subsidize her housing and other expenses. And they have taken her in when she has had no place else to go.

Several months ago, Mary was fired for repeated absenteeism and being intoxicated on the job, and she ended up moving back in with her parents. While there, she has been intoxicated much of the time, and they are afraid to leave her alone in the house. Given the circumstances, John and Evelyn have done no recreational traveling and almost no socializing in recent months.

At this point, John and Evelyn feel they cannot ask Mary to leave, since she has nowhere to go and could end up homeless on the streets or worse. Like any parents, their ultimate fear is that she will die unless they can do something. Their story of intellectual and emotional exhaustion, as well as a wrecked retirement, has created a feeling of utter helplessness. The counseling session ends with their plea for a new strategy to turn their daughter's life around.

Case Study 2: Beth and Her Family

Beth goes to a counselor to talk about her thirteen-year-old son, Mark. She appears tired and tense, but she is composed as she talks about her concerns. Mark has been acting out both in school and at church, and his religious education teacher has suggested that Beth might want to talk with a counselor about him. In fact, Beth is worried about the way Mark has been isolating himself from the rest of the family and even most of his friends. She also believes he has been experimenting with alcohol and marijuana.

When the counselor asks Beth about any other alcohol or marijuana use in the family, there is a painful silence and tears well up in her eyes. "Yes," she says, looking down and taking a deep breath. "Bill, my husband, is a very heavy drinker, and that makes it almost impossible for us to talk about Mark's problems, let alone to find some way to help him." The floodgates now open wide, and Beth tells a familiar story about the steady progression of Bill's drinking problem.

Five years ago, Bill was downsized out of an executive position in financial services. Although he found a new job within three months, during the interim, he became depressed and started drinking daily, occasionally passing out in front of the television at night. Then came the mood swings and erratic, often belligerent behavior, which began to disrupt the family's routine. Their efforts to control Bill's drinking with anger, threats, and pleading have had no effect on him.

Bill's drinking has affected his performance at work, too. He has lost two more jobs in recent years and now rarely leaves the house. Because of his unpredictability, the kids have stopped inviting their friends to their home. Beth no longer accepts friends' social invitations, and the entire family is constantly on edge trying not to upset him. It seems as though the family has turned in on itself, with all its energy and attention caught up in Bill's alcoholic behavior.

As more of her story pours out, Beth paints a painful picture of the desperation and slow disintegration of her family, their increasingly futile attempts to act normally in impossible circumstances, and the withering of her own self-confidence and self-esteem. Although she doesn't say it outright, it is clear that Beth is depending more and more on Mark's older sister Susan for both emotional support and help with some of the parenting role that Bill no longer performs. Although Beth has come to the counselor's office with concerns about her son, by the end of the meeting, the counselor recognizes that Beth is running out of strategies to cope with her life. Certainly, Bill is a candidate for assessment for chemical dependence, but the rest of the family is also in serious need of help to recover its own health and well-being.

While the details of these two family stories are different, the essential theme is identical: Efforts by family members of chemically dependent individuals to cope with the illness that is consuming their lives are highly debilitating and almost always ineffectual. Whether the illness has struck a parent, spouse, or child, the impact on the rest of the family (physical, emotional, spiritual) is remarkably similar.

Two critical points must be understood at this juncture. First, the addiction of one member of a family will inevitably have an impact on the lives of other family members and the family as a unit. Second, a lot can be done to help family members re-establish sanity and stability in their own lives, regardless of whether the chemically dependent individual recovers.

In both case studies, family members sought help because they had reached the end of their rope trying to change the behaviors of their chemically dependent loved one. That is, their primary purpose was *not* to get help for themselves. As pastoral caregivers, we can and should support them in responding to the presenting crisis, but the real opportunity is to help them recover their own lives, health, and well-being. The real opportunity is to help the family begin to heal.

The Family System

The composite family portraits presented in the preceding case studies show how the chemical dependence of a single family member affects other family members through their interpersonal relationships. Family systems theory is a useful tool for understanding this phenomenon. According to this theory, members of a family are not completely autonomous in their behaviors, emotions, and thinking. Says Murray Bowen, a founder of family systems theory, "The thoughts, feelings, and behavior of each family member . . . contribute to and reflect what is happening in the family as a whole." In a healthy system, there is a balance between individual autonomy and group togetherness.

Stress on the family, such as that caused by the erratic, self-centered, and hurtful behavior of a chemically dependent person, can increase the level of anxiety in the entire family. This will in turn increase the level of dependent, reactive behavior, which is not based on personal emotional needs but on the needs of another. As anxiety and stress grow, family members lose their capacity to care for themselves and to lead independent lives. The pathological energy at the family's core produces feelings of entrapment and loss of control, pulling family members deeper into seclusion and away from the help and objectivity that are available outside the family.

Once infected, the family system can become just as sick as the chemically dependent individual. And because of this, the family will not automatically be cured when the chemically dependent person is removed. Like the dependent person, the family, too, will often need treatment. What's more, sending a recovering individual home from treatment to an untreated family will rarely serve the recovery of anyone.

For the dysfunctional family to begin its journey back to health, it must escape the grip of self-centeredness and isolation and open itself up to a healing influence. By drawing family members out and turning their attention to self-care and a new, life-affirming direction, the pastoral caregiver can be that influence.

Codependency

When the family member of a chemically dependent person seeks the help of a pastoral caregiver, the caregiver is likely to encounter a confused and distraught individual with deep personal wounds. Whatever effects the drug or alcohol abuse has had on the family unit and the interrelationships within it, the caregiver's first concern must be the individual who has come to him or her.

Living with a drug- or alcohol-abusing person is traumatizing. Just talking with family members makes it readily apparent how their physical, emotional, and spiritual health has been damaged. Indeed, the resulting pattern of distortion in the family members' behavior, thinking, and feelings is so predictable that many psychologists have come to define the symptoms as a diagnosable personality disorder, popularly referred to as *codependency.*

Although codependency has not yet been universally accepted as a clinical entity, the concept has been widely used for diagnostic and treatment planning purposes in family addiction programs. But a caution is in order here: Just as an individual's drug or alcohol use can be characterized along a continuum from moderate social use to substance abuse (and with a lot of possibilities in between), so, too, the loved ones of a drug or alcohol abuser may experience a range of dysfunction.

Thus, the pastoral caregiver should be wary of pathologizing the distress of the family member who seeks help. Rather than reach for a clinical diagnosis, the caregiver may find it more useful (and true) to see the family member as someone who has tried to learn how to cope and survive in a very hostile environment and who has finally sought help because his or her attempts to fix the situation at home have been futile. Especially in a faith-based environment, it's important to encounter the whole person, exploring and supporting his or her emotional and spiritual strengths. Indeed, it is precisely the family member's spiritual resources (which are not typically well defined in any strictly clinical understanding of the problem) that may prove to be the key to his or her journey back to health and well-being.

While pastoral caregivers must be sensitive to the internal sources of the loved one's problems, as a practical matter, much of that individual's effort to regain emotional health will depend on cultivating a new, healthier relationship with the chemically dependent person and other family members. As much as anything else, such a relationship will flow from improved family communications, the logical focus of any family therapy.

Pastoral caregivers can learn several useful lessons from the recent work that has been done on so-called codependent personality disorder. According to Timmen Cermak, a pioneer in the development of criteria for diagnosing this disorder, several psychological problems are characteristic of codependency—a distorted relationship to willpower, confusion of identities, denial, and low self-esteem.

Thus, individuals who live with a drug or alcohol abuser often become committed to the belief that by exerting their own will, they will be able to control both their own behaviors and emotions and those of the substance abuser. This commitment can become all consuming. While these individuals may understand that in other areas of life, certain events and situations are beyond their control, they believe that they can prevail over the substance abuse problem in their family, if only they can exert sufficient willpower. As their attempts at control continue to fail, their sense of inadequacy increases and their sense of self-efficacy decreases. Ultimately, they fall into both isolation and hopelessness, thinking they can bring about change on their own if they just try harder, but they never succeed.

A fundamental understanding of codependency is that codependent individuals have an unhealthy dependence on others. In the case of substance abuse, they allow their self-worth to be defined by the behaviors and feelings of the substance-abusing loved one, thus relinquishing their separate identities. Their emotional and spiritual well-being become dependent on the emotional state of the drug or alcohol abuser.

This confusion or mixing of identities is what causes the uncontrollable "roller-coaster ride" experienced by the codependent person. When the drug- or alcohol-dependent person feels good and is doing well, the codependent person also feels good and does well. But when the chemically dependent person is upset and behaving inappropriately, the codependent person feels acute distress and responsibility for making him or her feel better and for stopping his or her hurtful behavior. Because neither is possible, the codependent person's commitment to persist in trying keeps him or her on the emotional roller coaster.

Chemically dependent people often use psychological defense strategies to maintain their addictive behavior in the face of mounting life problems. One such defense is *denial,* both of responsibility for the consequences of their self-destructive behavior or of the behavior itself. Family members also use denial, primarily to protect themselves against the realization that their loved one's behavior is beyond their control. If family members can attribute the chemically dependent person's self-destructive behavior to their own inability to correct it, then they can deny that a real problem exists and avoid seeking help. Thus, the denial of both the family members and their chemically dependent loved one perpetuate the dependent behaviors of both.

Feeling that they are held hostage by the unpredictable emotions and behaviors of the chemically dependent person and that their own attempts to exert control have proven ineffectual, family members eventually suffer the loss of self-efficacy and self-esteem. Given the self-imposed mission of fixing their chemically dependent loved one, they will know only failure and mounting hopelessness. Such troubled relationships inexorably erode family members' fundamental sense of their worth and dignity as human beings.

Assuming responsibility for meeting the chemically dependent person's needs while ignoring one's own represents another facet of codependent behavior. Abandoning one's own needs in the futile attempt to satisfy those of another person is often grounded in the fear of losing that person and being alone. This powerful need to be connected makes it likely that family members will be increasingly incapable of distinguishing their own needs and desires from those of the chemically dependent person.

The Role of the Pastoral Caregiver

Pastoral caregivers should be sensitive to family dynamics when family members seek their help in dealing with issues surrounding addiction. Helping troubled family members to reconnect with and honor their own needs should be a primary goal of pastoral care. If the caregiver is trained in family therapy techniques, that training can be brought to bear in working with family members. Even without formal training, however, caregivers can be sensitive to family dynamics in their pastoral work.

Family members are usually driven to seek help because of a crisis situation involving their chemically dependent loved one. And while a referral to formal family counseling may be in order, the pastoral caregiver's first priority should be to help them negotiate the situation at hand. The most likely scenario is that a single family member will seek help—usually but not always the spouse or partner of the chemically dependent individual. For whatever reason, that family member has finally realized the futility of his or her efforts to change the loved one's addictive behavior and has come seeking fresh ideas for ways to fix the individual. The family member may not acknowledge that the family unit needs help too; regardless, his or her description of the central problem will revolve around his or her personal ineffectiveness at changing the situation. Both the family member's personal problems and the specific nature of the current crisis should direct the pastoral caregiver's response.

The family member's immediate need is to be listened to with compassion and empathy. Seeking the counsel of a pastoral caregiver may represent his or her first step out of the darkness and chaos of the family environment but also the first painful and embarrassing exposure of the family secret. The family member needs to be welcomed without feeling judged. The caregiver must convey to the family member that he or she has come to a safe place, where he or she will find acceptance and understanding.

In one sense, the pastoral caregiver's challenge is to ensure that the family member will not retreat after this first pastoral encounter but feel comfortable enough to return for ongoing support and guidance. So, the caregiver should not view this encounter as an occasion for probing into the family's drug or alcohol history or for trying to change the family member's behavior toward his or her chemically dependent loved one. In fact, the first visit should be less about correcting attitudes and behaviors and more about establishing a trusting relationship, through which the family member can stay connected to the world beyond his or her family. A family member's reaching out represents his or her desire for spiritual reconnection with self, others, and the life force, and building a pastoral relationship that can foster these reconnections should be the first order of business. Indeed, nothing may be more important in the first pastoral encounter than setting a date for the next meeting.

In the process of intensive, responsive listening, the pastoral caregiver should encourage the family member to "let it all out," allowing him or her to be in touch with his or her feelings. This may be a new and frightening experience for the family member of a chemically dependent individual, who will have become accustomed to denying or otherwise controlling his or her emotions. Venting his or her anger and frustration toward the chemically dependent loved one may allow the family member to begin to identify his or her own needs. This in turn may provide an opening the caregiver can build on later and may lead to more effective coping in the home environment. To this end, the pastoral caregiver should postpone any discussion of the disease model of addiction during the first encounter. Being told that his or her loved one is ill may choke off the family member's healing expression of anger.

Beyond active, nonjudgmental, empathic listening, the pastoral caregiver should focus on the current situation—what prompted the family member's reaching out for help. The family member may be dealing with an episode of violence, the chemically dependent individual's loss of income, or disturbing behavior in a son or daughter. Whatever specifically prompted the visit should be addressed first, both because of its urgency to the family member and because education and counseling are likely to fall on deaf ears until the problem at hand has been resolved. Similarly, the first pastoral encounter may be too early to introduce the family member to a program such as Al-Anon. Making such a referral is unlikely to be meaningful until the family member is able to grasp his or her own need for help. But regardless of whether the family member participates in such a program or undertakes formal family therapy, ongoing pastoral encounters can productively focus on such topics as the nature of addiction and codependency, the importance of having an appropriate measure of detachment from the chemically dependent loved one's condition, and the need for a family recovery program.

Family Education

Substance abuse education is an indispensable component of any ongoing pastoral work with the family members of a chemically dependent individual. Through an understanding of both addiction and codependency, family members can begin to gain perspective on their family history and experience and understand the recovery process for themselves and their chemically dependent loved one. Simply naming the problem of addiction can lead to family members' recognizing patterns among the confusing and hurtful experiences that have characterized their lives. Shedding light on the family's destructive organizing principle, the addictive process, can help family members begin to make sense out of previously inexplicable experiences and tame unmanageable confusion and fears. Understanding that addiction is an illness can also help family members get beyond their self-blame and loss of self-efficacy.

One particular lesson in family education is worth emphasizing from the outset: There is no "quick fix" for addiction (or for codependent behavior). Professionals working from widely divergent models of addiction all agree that recovery from chemical dependence is a long process. Most consider it a life-long condition that cannot be cured but can be held in remission with diligent treatment and self-care. However it's defined, stable recovery is virtually never assured after a five-day stay in inpatient chemical detoxification or even a twenty-eight-day stay in an inpatient rehabilitation program. Daily attention to a carefully constructed treatment and aftercare plan must become a long-term commitment for the hope of recovery to be realistic. Thus, when a chemically dependent person undertakes a treatment and recovery program, his or her family's understanding of the recovery process and of their loved one's specific recovery plan will help determine how they should interact with him or her and what constitutes an appropriate level of support on their part (that is, a level of support that doesn't undermine their own recovery).

The Paradox of Detachment

In order for the family members of a chemically dependent individual to begin their own journey of healing, they must grasp this paradox: Their doomed attempts to be agents of change in their loved one's addictive life effectively keep him or her from getting the professional help that's needed. For instance, their failed attempts at change allow the chemically dependent individual to continue to manipulate them to maintain his or her addictive behavior. In addition, family members' failure to detach from the dependent person often leads to their making excuses for his or her destructive behaviors, effectively protecting him or her from experiencing the consequences of his or her addiction. It is precisely the cumulative impact of these experiences, often referred to as "hitting bottom," that prompts many people to change.

Grasping this important truth about the need for detachment is especially difficult for the parents of a chemically dependent adult or adolescent. They must grapple with the conflict between the parent's need to love unconditionally and protect his or her child and the chemically dependent individual's need for the motivation to change. That motivation will come in large part as the child is allowed to experience the negative consequences of addictive behavior. However, allowing youth to experience the consequences of their drug or alcohol experimentation does not mean turning a blind eye to such activity. Parents are legally and morally responsible for their underage children, and their involvement and intervention in any drug or alcohol use is critical to any attempt to correct dangerous behaviors.

Thus, the challenge for family members is twofold. First, they must give up responsibility for saving their chemically dependent loved one, including their efforts to stop or control the individual's drug or alcohol use. Second, family members must stop protecting the individual from the negative, painful consequences of his or her addictive behavior, thereby allowing that person to realize the motivation to get professional help. In letting go of their attachment to saving their loved one, family members can begin to attend to their own needs, which they have probably suppressed for a long time. The pastoral caregiver should emphasize that they need not wait for their loved one to get well to begin their own recovery.

For the healing process to begin, the family's status quo must be upset. Family members who seek help for *themselves* can provide an impetus for a change that affects all the other members of the family system, including the chemically dependent person. It is not unusual for a counselor who asks a chemically dependent client why he or she has decided to seek treatment at the given time to receive an answer like the following: "My wife [or husband] joined Al-Anon, and since then, it's been hell around the house." While pushing the chemically dependent individual into treatment should not be the reason family members seek help, it can definitely be one fortunate consequence.

It is important to remember that the family unit's healing does not depend on the sobriety of its chemically dependent loved one, and so that journey should not be delayed until the dependent person seeks help. In fact, family members' capacity to be appropriately supportive when the loved one does begin the recovery process will be very difficult if they have not begun to regain a measure of stability, independence, and centeredness in their own lives. As anger and resentment build within the family, respect and love for the chemically dependent individual inevitably diminish. In many cases, it is only through timely detachment that whatever remnant of love remains can be preserved.

Pastoral caregivers can promote the family's recovery by encouraging them to focus on their own plans and hopes for the future, which they probably abandoned in their compulsion to accommodate the needs of the chemically dependent individual. At first, such support may mean encouraging family members to do one thing every day that's just for themselves, such as get an ice-cream cone, take a luxuriant bath, or partake in an old hobby. The long process of reclaiming selfhood must begin with baby steps. Then, as self-efficacy and self-esteem build, more ambitious plans will come within reach.

In supporting family members' move to a new, more productive focus in their lives, the pastoral caregiver must help them understand that they are detaching from the addiction and addictive behaviors of their loved one, not from their care and concern for him or her. Separating the loved one from his or her illness is an essential teaching of Al-Anon, one that can help sustain the family's love for their sick family member. Likewise, this principle should be continually emphasized in pastoral care.

A final note to pastoral caregivers working with family members: Keeping families focused on their own needs and recovery can be quite difficult, especially in early pastoral sessions. If family members are allowed to fixate on saving the chemically dependent person, they will constantly push the conversation in that direction. This is something the caregiver should try to control.

Children

A sad but virtually inevitable consequence of untreated substance abuse in families is its harmful effect on the youngest family members. While some substance-abusing parents manage to function relatively normally in their parental role, many do not. The children of chemically dependent parents may display a range of physical, behavioral, and spiritual symptoms that stem from their dysfunctional home life. And if the recovery needs of these young people are overlooked, the result might be a lifetime of debilitating psychological and interpersonal problems.

Children can be affected by living in a household with a chemically dependent person in several ways. First, a chemically dependent parent often becomes incapable of fulfilling her or his parental role. That role may be assumed, in whole or in part, by the other parent (in a two-parent household), compromising the parent's primary role. An older sibling may also assume the chemically dependent parent's role in the family. Such role swapping is, at minimum, confusing to children and may lead to profound feelings of insecurity. It may, for instance, mean the loss of a primary gender role model, as formerly represented by the chemically dependent parent.

Second, the compulsive, unpredictable behavior of the dependent parent will distort his or her relationship with the child. The relationship may become unmanageable for the child and at the same time frighteningly inescapable. The relationship may become physically abusive, and the pastoral caregiver must be watchful for any signs of this development. In dysfunctional relationships with parents, children may find it difficult or impossible to find the security or approval they need for healthy development and emotional well-being. Life can become a nightmare of not knowing what's coming next or how to react.

Unfortunately, given these circumstances, the sober parent's availability for the child may be marginal at best. In fact, his or her relationship with the child may become equally disturbed, as he or she becomes ever more reactive to his or her partner's self-serving and destructive behavior. In trying to accommodate to or change that behavior, the sober parent often fails to offer protection, support, or guidance to the child. Effective parenting becomes very difficult, if not impossible. Indeed, the sober parent may turn to the child to meet his or her *own* emotional needs.

A fourth problem is that children, like other family members, are unlikely to seek outside help or support, even among peers. Indeed, a child's withdrawal from interactions with peers may signal that his or her life has been co-opted by addiction in the family. And so perhaps the ultimate threat to children in an addiction-disordered family is they may lose their childhood, as they and other family members assume inappropriate, self-destructive roles as demanded by the dysfunctional family system.

Pastoral caregivers can make a difference in the lives of children who attend church or church school in several ways. First, caregivers can pay particular attention to these children, displaying personal interest in their lives and concern for their well-being. In the process, caregivers can offer these children the opportunity for a stabilizing, caring relationship with an adult outside the family. Second, caregivers can support parents' efforts to detach from chemically dependent spouses or partners and to regain the capacity for effective parenting.

In addition, caregivers can work with families to encourage and support their children's participation in Alateen, a twelve-step program modeled on Al-Anon for children affected by a family member's chemical dependence. Caregivers should identify where the nearest Alateen meeting in the area is held and identify resources to help children attend. Alateen programs are frequently hard to find in many localities, so by hosting a meeting, the church can serve the larger community as well as its own children. Pastoral caregivers can also support families in choosing to include their children in family therapy or exploring the possibility of a child's own individual therapy.

Pastoral caregivers can support and encourage children's participation in the church's religious education program and other youth activities. In this regard, it may be helpful to personally introduce a child to specific teachers or youth group leaders who have been told in advance of the child's need for faith community connections. Of course, this should be done while respecting the confidentiality of the child's specific family situation.

As a practical matter, perhaps the most important contribution a pastoral caregiver can make to a codependent child's recovery is to help move his or her sober parent forward in the process of detachment and personal recovery. A child's hours in church are relatively few, and when all is said and done, his or her essential need is to have at least one stable and reliable parent. Again, if there are any signs of abuse, the pastoral caregiver may need to seek guidance and collaboration from local social service agencies for the protection of the child.

Programs for Families

In addition to any one-on-one pastoral care that a church can provide to family members of a chemically dependent person, there are several other initiatives that can support their healing and return to well-being. In particular, establishing a church support group for family members or close friends of chemically dependent individuals can serve several important functions:

- A support group can provide a safe place for people to express and begin to re-connect with their feelings. Unburdening themselves of the "family secret" can be a powerful experience; just holding the secret can be emotionally and spiritu-ally debilitating.
- As support group members realize they are in the company of people who share their range of experiences and emotions, they will not only find it easier to talk about their feelings but begin to connect with one another personally. This bonding will be one sign that family members have begun to break the chains of their isolation. Through these new relationships, family members will also likely get new perspective on their own situation, helping them see the possibility to grow beyond their addiction-centered life.
- By sharing their stories in a group committed to nonjudgmental support, family members can begin to diffuse the shame that often accompanies living in a chemically dependent family and regain their sense of dignity and self-worth.
- By connecting with the pain of others, the codependent person has the oppor-tunity to be caring without becoming entangled in these other people's lives. Relearning (or perhaps learning for the first time) healthy ways to care for others and to be cared for in return is critical to the recovery of emotional and spiritual balance. The challenge is to develop the capacity to serve others without losing sight of personal boundaries, the hallmark of codependent behavior.
- New group members can learn practical strategies for coping with their chemi-cally dependent loved ones from those further along in their recovery as they begin the process of detachment.
- Group members can support one another in their participation in Al-Anon, Alateen, and other twelve-step programs, wrestling together with any barriers they find to participation in such programs. Once again, the longer-term mem-bers of the group may have successful strategies to share with newer members.
- The interpersonal support work of the group may ease the way for group members to reconnect with other healing aspects of church life.

The family support group may or may not be led by a facilitator, depending on the preference and expectations of group members. If it's facilitated by someone with a background in family systems or substance abuse, the group can serve an educational as well as a supportive purpose. Developing and maintaining a sense of trust and safety among members should be a primary concern, and the dialogue should be conversational, not confrontational.

In launching a family support group, pastoral caregivers can encourage the participation of young adults. A support group with similar organization and goals can also profitably be started for children and adolescents; it will be critical to engage an adult facilitator for this type of group (or preferably two—one male and one female), with appropriate experience and sensitivities. A particularly rich environment is created when adult children, spouses/partners, and parents of chemically dependent individuals all participate. Such a group can lead to the formation of meaningful and lasting cross-generational relationships.

A critical reminder: While belonging to a church-based support group can augment participation in twelve-step recovery work (in this case, Al-Anon and Alateen), it should never be presented as an alternative to such participation.

The church can also make information on addiction, codependency, and recovery available to the family members of chemically dependent individuals. This information should include contacts for local family treatment services, literature on twelve-step groups (Al-Anon and Alateen, in particular) and their meeting times and locations, and general educational materials that explain the causes of chemical dependence, its signs and symptoms, the recovery process, and an overview of treatment approaches for both chemical dependence and family dysfunction. Such materials might include videos that could be used to focus discussions in family support groups.

Families are often in crisis when a family member finally seeks help, and this may be especially true if the chemically dependent individual is a parent and the breadwinner of the family. If this is the case, family income may be spotty or have dried up, routines of child care and household maintenance may be out of kilter, and the overall capacity of the family to carry on with its normal functioning may be severely impaired. Having the chemically dependent member placed in long-term residential care is likely to leave the family shorthanded and deprived of income. The pastoral caregiver can assess the family's practical needs and work through the addiction ministry committee or another church group set up for this purpose to help see the family through its immediate crisis. This support might entail arranging for day care or school transportation for the children, making meals, or assisting with household chores. Not only can such outreach provide essential, practical assistance to the family, but it will also further connect the family to the caring church community. In addition, the opportunity to provide such support can have profound meaning to church members who are in recovery themselves and who have progressed to the point where they can be of service to others.

The opportunity for recovering family members to serve other families or individuals in circumstances they have experienced or empathize with constitutes an essential component of all twelve-step recovery programs, passing along the caring and support that one has received from others. In addition to providing the opportunity for service work among its members, the church can expand service opportunities for family members to include the larger community. For instance, it can make arrangements with local social service agencies, schools, hospitals, drug and alcohol treatment programs, halfway houses, shelters, soup kitchens, and other organizations to provide volunteers where needed. There is no community in the United States that does not have an ongoing need for volunteers in the areas of addiction and family recovery.

Emerging from the pain and isolation of the chemically dependent family environment is daunting, and the people confronting this challenge are often beset by confusion and fear. Pastoral caregivers who are willing to accompany family members to their first Al-Anon meeting can help facilitate the transition into recovery. The companionship of these First Responders (see page 58) offers newly recovering family members additional opportunities to make healthy connections outside the family system and offers volunteer companions additional opportunities to serve.

Given that family members of chemically dependent people are more likely than chemically dependent individuals themselves to seek help in church settings, establishing the family-related components of the church's addiction ministry is no less important than responding to chemically dependent individuals. Both types of initiatives are critical to the long-term recovery prospects of church members whose lives have been affected by addiction.

Looking Forward

The conviction that underlies an addiction ministry is that a community of faith should be organized as a community of healing and growth toward life-affirming wholeness. The ideas presented in this work only begin to define the context in which new, abundant hope for recovery of spiritual well-being can be realized by people whose lives have been affected by addiction. If, in years to come, we find that these ideas have had only a small impact in their particulars but have had the larger effect of rededicating church communities as places of concern and support for healing from addiction, then this effort to define and implement addiction ministries will have proved worthwhile.

If your faith community has any experience reaching out to people touched by addiction or if this book prompts such an undertaking, I hope you will be in touch with us at the Center for Addictions Ministry (see the contact information provided below). We may be able to help you in your work. It is also our goal to grow as a central information resource. We want to hear about your ideas, programs, and experiences (successful and otherwise) so that we can share what you learn with others. Meanwhile, blessings on you and your work in this important ministry.

Center for Addictions Ministry
At First Parish Brewster
1 Harwich Road
Brewster, MA 02631
www.addictionsministry.org

Resources

Commonly Abused Substances

The information in this section on commonly abused substances is provided as a quick reference for pastoral caregivers, both for their own understanding and for their use in answering questions that may arise in counseling and other addiction ministry activities. This information may also prove useful as the content for drug and alcohol education and awareness sessions for people who routinely interact with children and adolescents. For further information, consult the websites and publications listed in the back of this book (see page 126).

Alcohol

Alcohol has been used by widely divergent cultures since the dawn of time as an intoxicant and a medicine. Beverage alcohol is *ethanol*, as distinguished from *methyl alcohol*, which is used as cooking fuel, and *isopropyl alcohol*, or rubbing alcohol. Beverage alcohol is derived by distillation (so-called hard liquor, such as vodka and whiskey) and fermentation (beer and wine) of yeast and various grains and fruit. One-and-one-half ounces of distilled spirits, one five-ounce glass of wine, and twelve ounces of beer (or wine cooler) contain approximately the same amount of pure ethanol (one-third ounce) and are considered the standard dosage units of beverage alcohol. For people who do not have a chemical abuse or dependence problem, moderate alcohol use (that is, up to two drinks per day for men and one per day for women and elderly individuals) is not considered to be harmful to health.

Some alcohol is absorbed through the stomach, but most is absorbed through the walls of the small intestine. Once alcohol has been absorbed, it's carried by the blood throughout the body to all of the organs and the brain. The brain, heart, and liver are particularly susceptible to the accumulation of alcohol, however.

Ethanol is broken down (or metabolized) at the rate of approximately one ounce in three hours; thus, a typical drink of beverage alcohol containing one-third of an ounce of ethanol is metabolized in approximately one hour. *Blood-alcohol concentration (BAC)* is the measurement of the weight of alcohol per volume of blood and is used to indicate how much alcohol a person has in his or her body at a given time. According to the National Highway Traffic Safety Administration, the allowed BAC limit for driving a car is 0.10 percent. The majority of states are now considering lowering the legal BAC limit to 0.08 percent. (Thirty states have already approved this new limit.) This 0.02 percent change in the BAC has been shown to significantly reduce the number of fatal auto crashes.

Intoxication effects: Emotional unpredictability, possible increased aggressiveness, talkativeness, lack of muscle coordination, slowed reaction time, decreased inhibitions, confusion, unsteady gait, slurred speech, sweating, nausea/vomiting, drowsiness, stupor, coma, seizures, heart irregularities, death.

Potential health consequences: Diseases of the liver, esophagus, brain, gastrointestinal tract, pancreas, cardiovascular system, and musculoskeletal system; cancer; tolerance; addiction.

Depressants

Also called *sedative hypnotics,* this category of drugs comprises substances that depress the central nervous system. It includes sleeping medications, antianxiety medications, including so-called minor tranquilizers (as distinguished from antipsychotic medications, or major tranquilizers, which are not central nervous system depressants), and new synthetic depressants, some of which are referred to as *club drugs* and *date-rape drugs.*

Rohypnol (flunitrazepam) is a long-acting benzodiazepine that is up to ten times stronger than Valium. While it is used in some countries to treat insomnia, it is not used medicinally in the United States. Instead, the drug is used by young people at so-called *raves* (all-night dance parties) and in dance clubs to induce a kind of drunken state. It has also become known as a date-rape drug, as it is sometimes used to sedate people without their knowledge in order to sexually assault them. The drug produces an effect like an alcoholic blackout; that is, while under its influence, the individual has use of his or her faculties, but as the drug wears off, he or she does not recall what happened under its influence. The drug GHB (gamma-hydroxybuterate) is similar to Rohypnol and also popular among young people.

Intoxication effects: Reduced pain and anxiety, feeling of well-being, lowered inhibitions, slowed pulse and breathing, lowered blood pressure, poor concentration, respiratory depression and arrest.

Potential health consequences: Confusion and fatigue; impaired coordination, memory, and judgment; addiction.

Cannabanoids

Cannabanoids include marijuana and hashish. Marijuana has been used for thousands of years in a variety of cultures and is today the most widely used illicit drug in the United States. The term *marijuana* refers to the flowering tops and leaves of the hemp (cannabis) plant. Marijuana is rolled into cigarettes or packed into hollowed-out cigars (*blunts*); it is also smoked in small pipes or larger water pipes called *bongs*. Marijuana users hold the smoke in their lungs for as long as possible to get the maximum effect.

There are more than sixty active ingredients in the cannabis plant, but THC (delta-9-tetrahydrocannabinol) is the ingredient considered to have the strongest effect on the brain. The average THC content of marijuana in 1997 was 5 percent, although the plant has been cultivated to have a THC content as high as 17 percent. The effects from smoking marijuana peak in approximately twenty to thirty minutes, and the intoxication can last up to three hours.

Chronic marijuana users, like heavy cigarette smokers, can develop respiratory problems, including a persistent, dry, hacking cough. Marijuana smoke also contains some of the same carcinogens as tobacco. Indeed, it has been estimated that smoking five marijuana joints a week delivers a roughly equivalent amount of carcinogens as smoking one pack of cigarettes a day. Despite the widespread belief that marijuana is not addictive, marijuana abuse and dependence occur, and both tolerance and withdrawal symptoms have been noted in marijuana users. While marijuana does not have the same toxic effects as other illicit drugs and is only moderately addictive, it can produce learning difficulties and a kind of apathy in young people that results in loss of ambition and other barriers to personal psychosocial development.

The number of marijuana users in the United States has declined steadily over the past twenty years, with roughly half the number of people using the drug today as in the 1970s. Still, an estimated 72 million Americans have used marijuana at least once. Marijuana is sometimes used in combination with other drugs, such as crack cocaine, PCP, and ketamine; the marijuana acts as a delivery mechanism for the other substance.

Hashish is made from resinous materials extracted from the cannabis plant and pressed into cubes or balls. Small pieces are broken or shaved off and smoked in pipes.

Intoxication effects: Euphoria, slowed thinking and reaction time, confusion, impaired balance and coordination.

Potential health consequences: Cough and frequent respiratory infections, impaired memory and learning, increased heart rate and anxiety; panic attacks, tolerance, addiction.

Dissociative Anesthetics

These substances, which include ketamine and PCP, constitute a small group of drugs that have hallucinogenic effects (sometimes classified as *hallucinogens*). Their use also causes the individual to feel detached or dissociated from his or her own identity and the environment. Interestingly, both PCP and ketamine were originally developed as anesthetics for use in humans and animals.

High doses of PCP can produce a profoundly altered state, including bizarre, violent behaviors and feelings of superhuman strength and invulnerability. Both PCP and ketamine can be used in combination with other drugs (for instance, users may dip marijuana in PCP before smoking it), and they are often sold at young people's dance clubs and raves. Although neither produces tolerance or withdrawal symptoms and neither is considered addictive, they are very dangerous chemicals and can cause long-term residual health problems (such as memory and speech disorders).

Intoxication effects: Increased heart rate and blood pressure, impaired motor function, numbness, nausea/vomiting, hypotension, seizure-like events, delerium, death.

Potential health consequences: Memory loss, speech disorders.

Hallucinogens

This category of abused drugs includes both synthetic substances and substances that occur naturally. The most widely used synthetic hallucinogen is LSD (lysergic acid diethylamide), which is also called *acid*. It is often made available in tiny tablets (*microdots*), clear squares (*windowpanes*), and as so-called blotter acid, in which the chemical is dripped or sprayed on absorbent paper that is ingested.

The dosages of LSD available today are much smaller than those used in the 1960s and have less severe effects, lasting up to twelve hours. However, LSD use has been associated with *flashbacks,* or recurrence of the drug's effects, sometimes months after drug use. LSD use has also produced such long-lasting conditions as depression and schizophrenia.

Mescaline is the psychoactive substance found in the crowns (or buttons) of peyote cactus plants. Peyote is used in some Native American spiritual practices.

Psilocybin is a mushroom that is eaten for its hallucinogenic effects. These effects are generally milder than those of LSD and mescaline and are often limited to disturbances in visual perception.

The predominant effect of the hallucinogens is heightened sensations and awareness. Users feel that their mental activity is enhanced, physical stimuli (such as sounds, odors, colors) seem sharpened or more vivid, and one's surroundings may seem distorted or disturbing. For instance, people often report losing a sense of the boundary between themselves and their surroundings. While hallucinogens can be abused and there is evidence of tolerance, there is no evidence of withdrawal symptoms.

Intoxication effects: Altered states of perception and feeling, nausea.

Potential health consequences: Chronic mental disorders, persisting perception disorder (flashbacks).

Opioids and Morphine Derivatives

The term *opioids* is used here to refer to both the drugs derived from opium-containing seeds of the poppy plant (such as morphine, heroin, and codeine) and to the synthetic, morphine-like drugs (such as fentanyl and methadone). The term *narcotic* is also used to refer to these drugs, but it is also used more loosely to mean any drug that can elicit abuse and dependence.

Opioid drugs cause depression of the central nervous system, sedation, and analgesia along with euphoria and a sense of well-being. They are used medicinally for pain relief and include such prescription analgesics as Vicodin (hydrocodone); Oxy-Contin, Percodan, and Percocet (oxycodone); Darvon (propoxyphene); Demerol (meperidine); and Dilaudid (hydromorphone). The synthetic drug methadone, which is used in the treatment of heroin dependence, is also included in this category. Methadone is dispensed in nonintoxicating dosages in maintenance programs to block both the high of heroin and the cravings it produces. It is also sold as a street drug.

People become addicted to opioids by abusing prescribed painkillers and through recreational use. Opioids can be taken by mouth, snorted, smoked, or injected. Dependence can result after only a few weeks of use, although dependence as a result of the therapeutic use of opioids for a short period of time is unusual (for example, in postoperative care). Such patients may exhibit tolerance and withdrawal symptoms, but they do not develop drug-seeking behavior or preoccupation with the drug.

Intoxication effects: Pain relief, euphoria, drowsiness, respiratory depression and arrest, nausea, confusion, constipation, sedation, unconsciousness, coma.

Potential health consequences: Tolerance, addiction.

Stimulants

The stimulants include cocaine, which is derived from the coca plant, and a number of synthesized chemicals, such as amphetamine. Nicotine, found in tobacco, is included in this category because of its predominantly stimulating effects on the brain and central nervous system. Nicotine has other effects on the brain as well, including a calming effect after stimulation, and other ingredients of tobacco have numerous harmful effects on the body.

Amphetamine and its several derivatives are used medicinally to treat obesity. The drug Ritalin (methylphenidate) is used to treat attention-deficit and hyperactivity disorders (ADHD). Methamphetamine is produced in clandestine laboratories. MDMA, or *Ecstasy,* has become popular with young people and is sold at dance clubs, parties, and raves. It is taken in pill form, and its effects can last from four to six hours. Among its serious effects are dehydration and an often dramatic elevation of body temperature. People who have died from overdoses of Ecstasy have been reported to have had core body temperatures as high as 109 degrees Fahrenheit.

Cocaine is used in powdered form, often laid out in *lines* and then snorted. It is also prepared in hard chunks, called *crack* or *freebase,* in which form it can be smoked in a pipe or dissolved and injected. In combination with heroin, it is called a *speedball* and is injected. Cocaine, especially when smoked, produces an intense euphoric rush that lasts only a few minutes. With repeated use, the intense highs are followed by equally intense lows marked by feelings of restlessness, anxiety, and depression; these feelings, along with the desired euphoria, become a stimulus for repeated use. Cocaine users often moderate the high of cocaine with the sedative effect of alcohol, a combination that is particularly toxic. In fact, the combined use of alcohol and cocaine is the most common cause of drug-related deaths, according to the National Institute on Drug Abuse.

Intoxication effects: Increased heart rate, blood pressure, and metabolism; feelings of exhilaration and energy; increased mental alertness; heart failure.

Potential health consequences: Rapid or irregular heartbeat, reduced appetite, weight loss.

Anabolic Steroids and Inhalants

Anabolic steroids are used to increase muscle size and strength and thus to enhance athletic performance and muscular appearance. They are abused for these effects rather than for intoxication.

Inhalants are widely available chemicals that are legal to purchase and relatively inexpensive and that produce a quick high. Their use can cause sudden death, due to irregular heart rhythms.

Jellinek's Phases and Progression of Alcoholism

Prealcoholic Phase
1. Occasional relief drinking
2. Constant relief drinking
3. Increase in alcohol tolerance

Prodromal Phase
4. Onset of blackouts
5. Surreptitious drinking
6. Increasing dependence on alcohol
7. Urgency of first drink
8. Feelings of guilt
9. Unable to discuss problem
10. Blackouts increase

Crucial Phase
11. Decrease of ability to stop drinking when others do so
12. Drinking bolstered with excuses
13. Grandiose and aggressive behavior
14. Persistent remorse
15. Efforts to control fail repeatedly
16. Promises and resolutions fail
17. Tries geographical escapes
18. Loss of other interests
19. Family and friends avoided
20. Work and money troubles
21. Unreasonable resentments
22. Neglect of food
23. Loss of ordinary willpower
24. Tremors and early-morning drinks
25. Decrease in alcohol tolerance
26. Physical deterioration

Chronic Phase

27. Onset of prolonged intoxications
28. Moral deterioration
29. Impaired thinking
30. Drinks with social inferiors
31. Indefinable fears
32. Unable to initiate action
33. Obsession with drinking
34. Vague spiritual desires
35. All alibis exhausted
36. Complete defeat admitted

Source: E. M. Jellinek, *The Disease Concept of Alcoholism* (New Haven, CT: Hill House Press, 1960).

The Twelve Steps of Alcoholics Anonymous

1. We admitted we were powerless over alcohol—that our lives had become unmanageable.
2. We came to believe that a Power greater than ourselves could restore us to sanity.
3. We made a decision to turn our will and our lives over to the care of God *as we understood Him.*
4. We made a searching and fearless moral inventory of ourselves.
5. We admitted to God, to ourselves, and to another human being the exact nature of our wrongs.
6. We were entirely ready to have God remove all these defects of character.
7. We humbly asked Him to remove all our shortcomings.
8. We made a list of all persons we had harmed and became willing to make amends to them all.
9. We made direct amends to such people wherever possible, except when to do so would injure them or others.
10. We continued to take personal inventory, and when we were wrong we promptly admitted it.
11. We sought through prayer and meditation to improve our conscious contact with God *as we understood Him,* praying only for knowledge of His will for us and the power to carry that out.
12. We have had a spiritual awakening as the result of these steps; we tried to carry this message to alcoholics and to practice these principles in all our affairs.

Source: Adapted from *Alcoholics Anonymous: The Story of How Many Thousands of Men and Women Have Recovered from Alcoholism,* 4th ed. (New York: Alcoholics Anonymous World Services, 1976), pp. 59–60.

Alcohol Abuse Assessment Tool

The CAGE questionnaire, which should be administered in an interview and not as a self-test, is a very simple yet highly reliable tool designed to identify people who are having problems with alcohol. It is composed of only four questions, which zero in on significant indicators of an individual's problem alcohol use. According to some substance abuse treatment providers, even one "yes" answer on the test suggests an alcohol problem. More generally, providing two or more "yes" answers is considered strong evidence of alcohol dependence. (In a test of its reliability, using two or more "yes" answers as indicative of alcohol dependency, the CAGE questionnaire identified 75 percent of the alcohol-dependent people who took the test.)

The CAGE Questionnaire

Have you ever:

- felt you should *C*ut down on your drinking?
- been *A*nnoyed by comments about your drinking?
- felt *G*uilty about your drinking?
- had an *E*ye-opener drink first thing in the morning?

Congregational Addiction Assessment Questionnaire

This questionnaire has been designed to help our congregation better understand the range and depth of addiction problems among our members and to learn what programs and services might be organized to address these problems. Your anonymous responses to the items in this questionnaire will help us prepare to reach out to those people at risk for or affected by addictive behavior, to support recovery and prevention, and to strengthen our ties to one another in community and to the spirit of life.

1. Are you concerned that you or someone important to you may have an addiction problem?   Yes ☐   No ☐

   • Are you concerned for yourself?   Yes ☐   No ☐

   • A family member?   Yes ☐   No ☐

   • Are you getting help for the problem?   Yes ☐   No ☐

   • Do you have a co-worker or friend with an addiction problem that is affecting *your* life?   Yes ☐   No ☐

   • Are you getting help dealing with these friends or loved ones?   Yes ☐   No ☐

   • Do you need help finding out if there is a problem?   Yes ☐   No ☐

   • What addictive substances or behaviors are affecting your life or the life of a loved one? Check all that apply:

     Drugs (illegal or prescription) ___   Alcohol ___   Food ___   Sex ___

     Gambling ___   Internet ___   Other (please specify) _____

2. Would you or someone you know be interested in (check appropriate boxes):

   • A support group within our congregation for:

     _____ people in early recovery from drug or alcohol dependence?

     _____ family and friends of substance-dependent individuals?

     _____ teenagers dealing with their own addiction or that of family or friends?

- Adult education programs focusing on:

  _____ the nature of chemical dependence and how to identify a problem?

  _____ facts and myths about drugs and alcohol?

- short-term addiction assessment and referral?

- faith-based addiction counseling?

3. Would you like to see more attention to drugs and alcohol in the religious education program? Yes ☐ No ☐

4. Would you like to see addiction and recovery addressed in worship services? Yes ☐ No ☐

   If so, how often? Once a year _____ Twice a year _____ Four times a year _____

5. Would you attend a worship service held at a designated time that focused on recovery issues? Yes ☐ No ☐

6. Please note any comments or questions below.

For More Information

Websites

Al-Anon/Alateen: www.al-anon.alateen.org

Alcoholics Anonymous (AA): www.alcoholics-anonymous.org

Hazelden Foundation: www.hazelden.org

National Association for Children of Alcoholics (NACOA): www.nacoa.net

National Clearinghouse for Alcohol and Drug Information (NCADI): www.health.org

National Council on Alcoholism and Drug Dependence (NCADD): www.ncadd.org

National Institute on Alcohol Abuse and Alcoholism (NIAAA): www.niaaa.nih.gov

National Institute on Drug Abuse (NIDA): www.nida.nih.gov

Substance Abuse and Mental Health Services Administration (SAMHSA): www.samhsa.gov

Books

Alcoholics Anonymous: The Story of How Many Thousands of Men and Women Have Recovered from Alcoholism. 4th ed. New York: Alcoholics Anonymous World Services, 2001.

Apthorp, Stephen P. *Alcohol and Substance Abuse: A Clergy Handbook.* Wilton, CT: Morehouse-Barlow, 1985.

Beattie, Melody. *Codependent No More: How to Stop Controlling Others and Start Caring for Yourself.* New York: Harper/Hazelden, 1987.

Clinebell, Howard. *Understanding and Counseling Persons with Alcohol, Drug, and Behavioral Addictions: Counseling for Recovery Using Psychology and Religion.* Rev. ed. Nashville: Abingdon Press, 1998.

Falkowski, Carol. *Dangerous Drugs.* Center City, MN: Hazelden, 2000.

Fuad, Margaret A. *Alcohol and the Church: Developing an Effective Ministry.* Pasadena, CA: Hope, 1992.

How Al-Anon Works for Families and Friends of Alcoholics. Virginia Beach, VA: Al-Anon Family Group Headquarters, 1995.

Jellinek, E. M. *The Disease Concept of Alcoholism.* New Haven, CT: Hill House Press, 1960.

Johnson, Vernon E. *I'll Quit Tomorrow: A Practical Guide to Alcoholism Treatment.* New York: HarperCollins, 1990.

————. *Intervention: How to Help Someone Who Doesn't Want Help.* Minneapolis: Johnson Institute, 1986.

Julien, Robert M. *A Primer of Drug Action.* 6th ed. New York: W. H. Freeman, 1992.

Kabat-Zinn, Jon. *Wherever You Go There You Are.* New York: Hyperion, 1994.

Kasl, Charlotte Davis. *Many Roads, One Journey: Moving Beyond the Twelve Steps.* New York: HarperCollins, 1992.

Keller, John. *Ministering to Alcoholics.* Minneapolis: Augsburg, 1966.

Kinney, Jean, and Gwen Leaton. *Loosening the Grip: A Handbook of Alcohol Information.* 5th ed. St. Louis: Mosby/Year Book, 1995.

Kus, Robert J., ed. *Spirituality and Chemical Dependency.* Binghamton, NY: Harrington Park Press, 1995.

Living Sober. New York: Alcoholics Anonymous World Services, 1975.

May, Gerald G. *Addiction and Grace.* New York: HarperCollins, 1988.

McGurrin, Martin C. *Pathological Gambling: Conceptual, Diagnostic, and Treatment Issues.* Sarasota, FL: Professional Resource Press, 1992.

McKeever, Bridget Clare. *Hidden Addictions: A Pastoral Response to the Abuse of Legal Drugs.* Binghamton, NY: Haworth Pastoral Press, 1998.

Merrill, Trish. *Committed, Caring Communities: A Congregational Resource Guide for Addictions Ministries.* Austin: Texas Conference of Churches, 1994.

Phillip Z. *A Skeptic's Guide to the 12 Steps.* Center City, MN: Hazelden, 1990.

Prochaska, James O., John C. Norcross, and Carlo C. Diclemente. *Changing for Good.* New York: Avon Books, 1994.

Royce, James E. *Alcohol Problems and Alcoholism: A Comprehensive Survey.* Rev. ed. New York: Free Press, 1989.

Schaef, Anne Wilson. *Co-Dependence, Misunderstood, Mistreated.* San Francisco: Harper and Row, 1983.

Vaillant, George E. *The Natural History of Alcoholism Revisited.* Cambridge, MA: Harvard University Press, 1995.

Acknowledgments

Many people have contributed, knowingly and unknowingly, to the realization of this book—some through the inspiration of their lives and work, others through their insights into the extraordinarily complex subject of addiction, and still others through their understanding of addiction's spiritual ground.

Here, I want to single out my teachers: Drs. Howard Shaffer, Emil Chiauzzi, and Jan McCarthy and Revs. Brita Gill-Austern, Jerry Handspicker, and Gerald Krick.

At First Parish Brewster, I am indebted to so many, but I especially want to acknowledge Revs. Jim Robinson, Myke Johnson, and Pancheta Peterson; Carol Ann Yeaple; and Victoria Saper and the other members of FPB's Addictions Ministry Committee.

In three topical areas of this book, I am particularly indebted to the research and writing of others in the development of my own ideas on the subjects. Thus, I wish to acknowledge the influence of Howard Clinebell's ideas on working with families touched by addiction, Yifrah Kaminer's work on substance abuse in adolescents, and William R. Miller's insights into the important issue of surrender versus control as it bears on recovery from substance abuse.

The thread of constancy through all my work has been the support, encouragement, spiritual insight, and editing skills of my wife and soulmate, Janet Meacham.

Finally, I am indebted to all my clients and profoundly grateful that they have invited me into their lives.

Index

AA. *See* Alcoholics Anonymous
Adams, J. L., 18
Addiction. *See also* Dependence
   definition of, 8, 9
   spiritual component of, 19. *See also*
      Spirituality
   terminology of, 2–3, 8, 9, 9
Addiction ministry committee (AMC), 47–64
   education of, 50–51
   establishment of, 42, 47, 48, 64
   goals of, 50
   limitations of, 48–49
   meetings of, 49
   membership of, 42, 47–49
   pastoral caregivers' roles in, 48. *See also*
      Pastoral caregivers
   pastor's role in, 47–48
   programs of, 50, 52–64, 75–78
   purposes of, 42, 48–50
   women in, 83
Addiction resource center, 55–58, 77, 83,
   107
Adolescent problem drinking, 67. *See also*
     Children and adolescents, alcohol and
     drug use by
Adolescent Substance Abuse (Kaminer), 72

Adolescents. *See* Children and adolescents
Adult education, 53–54. *See also* Parents,
     education and awareness of
AIDS/HIV, 50, 56
Al-Anon, 15, 55, 61, 63, 83, 101, 103, 105,
   106, 107, 108
Alateen, 15, 55, 63, 105, 106, 107
Alcohol use/abuse, 113–114. *See also* Substance
     use/abuse
   by children and adolescents. *See* Children
     and adolescents
   church policy regarding, 63, 78
   deaths from, 4, 66, 68, 84
   by elderly individuals. *See* Elderly
     individuals
   fetal alcohol syndrome and, 79
   genetics as risk factor for, 70
   incidence of, 3–4, 23
   physical abuse and, 79–80
   progression of, 6–7. *See also* Models
   by women. *See* Women
Alcoholics Anonymous (AA), 13–16
   availability of, 14
   "Big Book" of, 15, 22, 23, 24–25, 29, 56
   children and adolescents and, 67, 73
   elderly individuals and, 90–91

Alcoholics Anonymous *(continued)*
    family programs of, 15. *See also* Al-Anon;
        Alateen
    higher power and, 24–30
    history of, 13, 26
    literature of, 15, 25, 27, 55
    meetings of, 14, 25–26, 28, 37–38, 55, 63
    membership of, 13, 14, 66–67
    principles of, 14–16, 19
    religious overtones of, 15–16, 24–25
    service component of, 14, 30, 47
    spiritual component of, 15–16, 22–30,
        38
    sponsorship in, 14–15
    success of, 22, 23, 47
    support groups and, 61
    Twelve Steps of, 14, 23–30, 122
Alcoholics Anonymous: The Story of How Many
    Men and Women Have Recovered from
    Alcoholism, 15, 56
Alcoholism (Estes and Heinemann), 85
Alternative medicine, 32
AMC. *See* Addiction ministry committee
American Academy of Pediatrics, 67
American Medical Association, 9
Amphetamines, 118
Anabolic steroids, 119
Attachment (and addiction), 19–20, 21.
    See also Spirituality

BAC. *See* Blood-alcohol concentration
"Big Book" (of Alcoholics Anonymous), 15,
    22, 23, 24–25, 29, 56
Blood-alcohol concentration (BAC), 86,
    113–114
Bowen, M., 96–97
Buddy system, 89

CA. *See* Cocaine Anonymous
CAGE questionnaire, 54, 123
Califano, J., 66
Cannabanoids, 115–116. *See also* Marijuana
Case studies, 28, 94–96
Cermak, T., 98
CHARM questionnaire, 88

Children and adolescents, 66–78
    abuse of, 105
    alcohol and drug use among, 3, 4, 8, 14, 40,
        66–67
    experimentation by, 67, 69, 77, 82
    faith communities and, 40, 52–54, 75–78
    families of, 70, 71–72, 104–105. *See also*
        Family and friends
    genetics and, 70, 71–72
    mental health issues of, 69–70, 74
    multiple-drug use among, 8, 14, 66–67, 74
    pastoral caregivers' contact with, 74–78, 105
    peer groups of, 71
    personality issues of, 70–71
    progression of substance use in, 72–73
    protective factors for substance abuse,
        71–72
    relationships with parents, 70, 71–72,
        104–105
    religious education for, 52–54, 76–77, 78,
        82, 105
    risk factors for substance abuse, 68–71
    of substance-dependent parents, 3, 80, 84,
        104–105
    treatment approaches for, 67, 73–74, 105
Church staff/committees, 52, 54–55.
        See also Faith communities; Pastoral
        caregivers
Churches. *See* Faith communities
Club drugs, 114
Cocaine, 117, 118
Cocaine Anonymous (CA), 13, 55
Codeine, 117
Codependency, 27, 60, 97–99, 105. *See also*
    Children and adolescents; Family and
    friends
Columbia University, Center on Addictions
    and Substance Abuse, 66
Committed, Caring Communities (Merrill), 3
Community, 36, 37, 38–39, 45. See also *Faith*
    communities
Congregational needs assessment, 61–62,
    124–125
Crack, 118
Craving, 3

Date-rape drugs, 114
Denial, 7–8, 11, 44, 99
Dependence. *See also* Addiction
    definition of, 2, 8, 9
    diagnosis of, 7–9
    models of. *See* Models
    physiology of, 2–3, 6
    as topic of worship service, 63
    treatment and recovery from. *See* Treatment
        and recovery
Depressants, 114
Depression, 79, 87–88
Detachment, 102–103
Diagnosis (of chemical dependence), 7–8, 22
Disabled individuals, 50, 57
Disease Concept of Alcoholism, The (Jellinek), 6
Dissociative anesthetics, 116
Dowling, E., 26
Drug use/abuse. *See also specific drugs*
    by children and adolescents. *See* Children
        and adolescents
    deaths from, 84
    by elderly individuals. *See* Elderly
        individuals
    incidence of, 3–4, 23
    progression of, 5–7. *See also* Models
    treatment for. *See* Treatment and recovery
    by women. *See* Women
Dynamics of Faith (Tillich), 20
Dysfunctional families, 96–97. *See also* Family
    and friends

Elderly individuals, 84–91
    alcohol and drug use by, 41, 84–89
    assessment of, 84–85, 86–88
    faith communities and, 41, 89–91
    family and friends of, 88, 91
    health issues of, 84, 85–88
    lifestyle of, 87–88, 89–91
    mental health issues of, 87–88
    pastoral caregivers' contact with, 84–85, 87,
        88, 89–91
    risk factors for substance abuse, 87–88
    tolerance by, 86–87
    treatment approaches for, 89

Estes, N., 85
Exercise, 33, 45

Faith communities
    alcohol and drug use within, 61–62,
        124–125
    children and adolescents in, 40, 52–54,
        75–78
    collaboration among, 63–64, 78
    elderly individuals in, 41, 89–91
    families in, 106–108
    parents in, 41
    recovery in, 39–42, 45–46. *See also*
        Treatment and recovery
    sponsorship of twelve-step programs by, 15,
        63, 83
    value of participation in, 36, 37, 39, 45
    women in, 82–84
Family and friends, 93–108
    of children and adolescents, 70, 71–72,
        104–105
    codependency among, 27, 60, 97–99, 105
    detachment by, 102–103
    of elderly individuals, 88, 91
    education and awareness of, 54, 101–102
    effects of dependence on, 3, 93–96
    faith communities and, 106–108
    genetics as risk factor for, 70, 71–72
    husband/wife relationships and, 79, 81,
        83
    model of family systems, 96–97
    parent/child relationships and, 70, 71–72,
        104–105
    pastoral caregivers' contact with, 44–45,
        98–101, 102, 103–104, 106–108
    support groups for, 106–107
    treatment approaches for, 15, 99–100,
        103–108
Family systems theory, 96–97
Family therapy techniques, 99–100
Fetal alcohol syndrome, 79
First Responders, 58–60, 83, 108
Foege, W., 4
Frankl, V., 18
Friends. *See* Family and friends

Galanter, M., 3
Gamblers Anonymous (GA), 13
Gateway theory, 72
Gender issues, 78–79, 80–81. *See also* Women
Genetics and alcoholism, 70, 71–72

Hallucinogens, 116–117
Hashish, 115
Hazelden Foundation, 56
Health and healing
    of children and adolescents, 69–70, 74
    community and, 38–39, 45–46. *See also*
      Faith communities
    of elderly individuals, 84, 85–88
    exercise and, 33, 45
    focus of, 31–32. *See also* Treatment and
      recovery
    history of, 31
    mental well-being, 69–70, 74, 79–80,
      87–88
    nutrition and, 33, 45, 89
    traditional approaches to, 32
Heinemann, M. E., 85
Heroin, 117
Higher power, 24–30
HIV/AIDS, 50, 56
Honesty, 30, 34
How Al-Anon Works for Family and Friends of
    Alcoholics (Al-Anon), 56
Humor, 33

Inhalants, 119
Interventions, 44–45. *See also* Treatment and
    recovery

Jellinek, E. M., 6–7, 54, 120–121
Johnson, V. E., 5–6, 7, 20
Journal of the American Medical Association, 4
Jung, C., 23

Kabat-Zinn, J., 34–35
Kaminer, V., 72, 74
Kinney, J., 4
Kleber, H., 3

Leaton, G., 4
Life strategies (for long-term recovery),
    33–36
Loosening the Grip (Kinney and Leaton), 4
Lord's Prayer, 25
Loved ones. *See* Family and friends
Lowinson, J., 79, 80
LSD (Lysergic acid diethylamide), 116–117
Lysergic acid diethylamide. *See* LSD

Man's Search for Meaning (Frankl), 18
Marijuana, 72, 115–116
McGinnis, J., 4
Meditation, 34, 45
Mental health issues
    of children and adolescents, 69–70, 74
    of elderly individuals, 87–88
    of women, 79–80
Merrill, T., 3
Methamphetamine, 118
Mindfulness movement, 34–35
Models (of substance use/abuse)
    for children and adolescents, 72–73
    disease model, 9–10, 31–32, 101–102
    family systems theory, 96–97
    Jellinek model, 6–7, 54, 120–121
    Johnson model, 5–6, 7, 20
    spiritual progression of dependence model,
      20–22
    stages of change model, 10–13
Morphine derivatives, 117–118
Mortality, 17–18
Mothers, 79, 80, 84. *See also* Parents
Multiple-drug use/abuse, 8, 14, 66–67, 74

NA. *See* Narcotics Anonymous
Narcotics, 117. *See also* Opioids
Narcotics Anonymous (NA), 13, 55, 63
National Council on Alcoholism and Drug
    Dependence, 3, 4, 66
National Highway Traffic Safety
    Administration, 113–114
National Institute for Alcohol Abuse and
    Alcoholism, 67

Nicotine, 118
Nutrition, 33, 45, 88

OA. *See* Overeaters Anonymous
Opioids, 117–118
Overeaters Anonymous (OA), 13, 55, 63

Parents
    education and awareness of, 40, 52–53,
        76
    faith communities and, 41
    relationships with children, 70, 71–72,
        104–105
    substance dependence by, 3, 80, 84,
        104–105
    support groups for, 76
Pastoral caregivers, 42–44, 47–51. *See also*
        Addiction ministry committee
    acceptance by, 12–13
    assessment made by, 9, 13, 97, 98
    children's and adolescents' contact with, 40,
        52–54, 75–78
    companionship provided by, 32
    crisis management by, 42, 43, 44, 100,
        107–108
    education of, 7, 23, 43, 44, 48, 49–50
    elderly individuals' contact with, 84–85, 87,
        88, 89–91
    families' contact with, 44–45, 98–101, 102,
        103–104, 106–108
    holistic perspective of, 33, 45–46
    initial contact with, 9, 42, 43, 44–45,
        100
    limitations of, 43, 44, 48–49, 51
    motivation provided by, 7, 13, 15–16, 26,
        27, 32, 43
    referrals made by, 9, 42–43, 44, 45, 48–49,
        51, 74, 76, 101
    resources available to, 57
    teaching provided by, 49–50, 52–55, 57
    women's contact with, 78–79, 80, 81,
        82–84
Pastors, 47–48
Peer groups, 71

Personal interests/hobbies, 34, 45, 90
Personality issues, 70–71
Physical abuse, 79–80, 105
Polysubstance use/abuse, 8, 14. *See also*
        Multiple-drug use/abuse
Prayer, 25, 28, 34, 45
Pregnancy, 79
Prescription medications, 79, 85, 88, 117
Problematic substance use, 8, 9. *See also*
        Substance use/abuse
Prochaska, J., 10–12

Religious education, 52–54, 76–77, 78, 82,
        105

Secondary prevention, 53, 63
Secular Organizations for Sobriety (SOS), 16,
        55
Secular Sobriety Groups (SSG), 16
Sedative hypnotics, 114
Serenity Prayer, 28
Service to others
    as principle of AA, 14, 30, 47
    satisfaction derived from, 34, 47
Shoemaker, S. M., 26
SMART Recovery, 16
Smith, B., 13
SOS. *See* Secular Organizations for Sobriety
Special populations (and substance use/abuse),
        65–91
    children and adolescents, 66–78. *See also*
        Children and adolescents
    disabled individuals, 50
    elderly individuals, 84–91. *See also* Elderly
        individuals
    HIV/AIDS individuals, 50, 56
    pastoral caregivers and, 65. *See also* Pastoral
        caregivers
    treatment approaches for, 65. *See also*
        Children and adolescents, treatment
        approaches for; Elderly individuals,
        treatment approaches for; Women,
        treatment approaches for
    women, 78–84. *See also* Women

Spirituality (and addiction)
   attachment and, 19–20, 21
   faith and, 18, 24, 45–46
   model of, 20–22
   mortality and, 17–18, 90
   surrender and, 24–30, 83–84
SSG. *See* Secular Sobriety Groups
Stages of change model, 10–13
Stigmatization, 4, 8, 9–10, 37–38, 50, 51,
      80–81, 84, 89
Stimulants, 118
Substance Abuse (Lowinson), 79
Substance use/abuse. *See also* Alcohol
      use/abuse; Drug use/abuse
   chronic nature of, 12, 101–102
   history of, 2, 3, 9
   incidence of, 3–4
   terminology of, 2–3, 8, 9, 67, 69
   levels of, 8
   progression of, 5–7. *See also* Models
   prevalence of, 3–4, 23, 33
   reasons for, 1–2, 4–7, 9. *See also* Models
   research on, 65, 67, 78
   stigma about, 4, 8, 9–10, 37–38, 50, 51,
      80–81, 84, 89
   as topic of worship service, 63
   treatment and recovery from. *See* Treatment
      and recovery
Support groups, 60–61, 76, 82, 106–107

Teachers, 53. *See also* Pastoral caregivers,
      teaching provided by
Telescoping (in substance abuse), 79
Textbook of Substance Abuse Treatment (Galanter
      and Kleber), 3
Tillich, P., 20
Tobacco, 118
Tolerance, 3, 86–87
Transcendental awareness, 35
Treatment and recovery
   availability of programs, 4, 14, 56
   of children and adolescents, 67, 73–74, 105.
      See also Children and adolescents

of elderly individuals, 89. *See also* Elderly
      individuals
faith communities and, 39–42, 45–46.
      See also Addiction ministry committee
of families, 15, 99–100, 103–108. *See also*
      Family and friends
programs for, 13–16, 39–40, 41–42. *See also*
      specific programs
of special populations, 65. *See also* Special
      populations
spiritual component of, 22–30
strategies for, 33–36, 39–40
of women, 81. *See also* Women
Twelve-step programs. *See* Alcoholics
      Anonymous; Treatment and recovery,
      programs for

Violent crime, 80

Wherever You Go There You Are (Kabat-Zinn),
      34–35
Wilson, B., 13, 23, 26
Withdrawal, 3
Women, 78–84
   alcohol and drug use by, 78–80, 86
   assessment of, 80–81
   faith communities and, 82–84
   gender differences and, 78–79, 80–81
   medical research and, 78
   mental health issues of, 79–80
   as mothers, 79, 80, 84
   pastoral caregivers' contact with, 78–79, 80,
      81, 82–84
   physical abuse of, 79–80
   pregnancy by, 79
   risk factors for substance abuse, 78–79
   stigmatization of, 80–81, 84
   treatment approaches for, 81
   violent crime and, 80
   as wives, 79, 81, 83